D1826672

John Montgomery is a highly respected and broadly networked leader in our area. He is passionate for the cause of Christ and His church. I count it an honor to be his colleague and friend.

—Joel C. Hunter, DMin
Senior Pastor
Northland—A Church Distributed

The author has been a close friend of mine for more than forty years. I have always felt he had a book in there somewhere. His sense of humor as he approaches the subject of stress is unparalleled. John is witty, clever, insightful, smart (not brilliant, just smart), and always has something worthwhile to say. I never have figured out whether John is a banker–businessman inside a minister, or a minister inside a banker–businessman. He is a unique individual.

—Blair Culpepper
Retired banker, board member
First National Bank of Central Florida

I have known John Montgomery as a pastor, leader, and mentor for more than thirty years. His words, character, and godly handling of stressful situations have taught me much. I can think of no better person to write a book on this subject and believe many will benefit from his wisdom and experience.

—Rick Harper
Pastor, StoneBridge Church
Charlotte, North Carolina

John Montgomery's life is an example of a type of life that one should strive to live. He is a man who has consistently shown integrity and has a wonderful sense of humor. In his first book, he tackles the difficult issue we all face in life: stress. This is accomplished as a result of years of acquired wisdom obtained through the exposure to peoples' needs, which he has treated with open arms and a caring heart. All this is fueled through his solid Christian belief, which is evident in his book, from the pulpit every Sunday, and most importantly, in his everyday walk through life.

—Michael Bougoulias, MD
Partner, Physician Associates

I know Pastor John Montgomery to be not only a spiritual leader within our community but a true practitioner of what I consider to be faith. His outlook always accentuates the positive and conveys to those facing whatever the challenge or event that they are not alone in their journey. His God-given personality generates a sense of calmness, which I have observed firsthand, and an immediate diffusion of tensions.

—John C. Litton
City Manager
Lake Mary, Florida

There are not two less likely people to have become friends than John Montgomery and I, yet I have spent more than fifteen years admiring and often wishing to be more like him. His words of counsel have served me well, but more cherished than his good advice has been his presence in the midst of my storm-filled life. He has provided me safe haven, acceptance, and saving grace. Anyone who knows John or reads his words will find a peace that is hard to understand yet is as real as the wind upon your face.

—Clint Kemp
Retired Pastor, New Providence Community Church
Nassau, Bahamas

I have known John Montgomery since the seventies when he was moving from the business/financial world into full-time ministry. As a Christian businessman I appreciate that, in addition to his many other talents, John brings personal experience from both spheres to all he does.

—Ray Good
Elder at Knox Presbyterian Church in Minneapolis and
former executive with Heinz America, Munsingwear, and
Pillsbury

Dr. John Montgomery

Sick of Stress

CREATION
H O U S E
A STRANG COMPANY

SICK OF STRESS by Dr. John Montgomery
Published by Creation House
A Strang Company
600 Rinehart Road
Lake Mary, Florida 32746
www.creationhouse.com

Scripture quotations are from the Holy Bible, New International Version. Copyright © 1973, 1978, 1984, International Bible Society. Used by permission.

The author wishes to acknowledge the great benefit toward his understanding of Song 23 due to Philip Keller's *A Shepherd Looks at Psalm 23*.

Design Director: Bill Johnson

Cover designer: Terry Clifton

Library of Congress Control Number: 2008939240

International Standard Book Number: 978-1-59979-490-7

First Edition

08 09 10 11 12 — 987654321

Printed in the United States of America

Dedication

This book is dedicated to the queen of the angels, my wife, Linda, who helps me stress less.

Contents

Foreword ix

Preface xi

Acknowledgments xiii

Introduction xv

Part I: Leading Stressors

1 Personal Issues 2

2 Health Issues 5

3 Life Issues 6

Part II: Leading Symptoms

4 Mind 15

5 Body 17

6 Spirit 21

Part III: Leading Stress Solutions

7 *S* is for Spirituality 28

8 *T* is for Time 30

9 *R* is for Relationships 37

10 *E* is for Escape 42

11 *S* is for Spending 47

12 *S* is for Shepherd 53

Afterword 75

Conclusion 77

Notes 78

About the Author 80

To Contact the Author 81

Foreword
Stress!

If you don't deal with stress, I want to do you a favor. If you're looking at this book, put it down right now. If you just bought it, take it back to the clerk. If you ordered it, send it back.

You will save money and then you'll owe me.

Go ahead.

Now for those of you who are honest, are not living in denial, do not live on Mars, and are sober, let me welcome you to a book that is going to make a difference in your life. And not only that, it's a book written by someone who lives what he writes.

John Montgomery has been my pastor, my colleague in ministry, my regular "go to" person for wisdom and insight, and my friend for over thirty years. That means I've watched him for a very long time and in a great variety of circumstances.

I was around John when his life and ministry had gone through enough pressure to make someone else leave the Christian faith and become a Buddhist. I've seen how he fathered his children, loved his wife, and led his congregation. I've watched as he reached out to people who were broken, afraid, and sometimes suicidal. I've listened to him preach and teach, and watched him answer questions and correct error, and I can't think of anybody else who speaks on the subject of stress and how to handle it with more credibility and wisdom.

I may be the most cynical person you've ever met. If someone gave me a book about how to handle stress, frankly, I would probably burn it. Do you know why? Because the odds are that the book was written to either "hustle a buck" or enhance a reputation, or by someone who is stressed out and thought that, by writing about it, they might find a way to deal with their own stress.

John Montgomery is the real deal. He is the kind of friend who you want to hold the rope when you're hanging over a cliff. You know he won't smell the flowers, think of something else, or let go. He'll hang on to the rope and pull you up. And then, more important for the subject of this book, when you are on safe ground standing next to John, you'll sense that things are going to be OK.

John Montgomery is one of those people who "carry their calm" with them wherever they go. And he's the kind of guy who makes you feel calm when you're around him. I've been the recipient of that gift on several occasions and, as one who carries his stress with him, I've often wondered how he did it.

Now I know and you are about to find out.

I commend this book and its author to you. Read it and be glad that the author took the time to write it down.

—Steve Brown
Reformed Theological Seminary
Orlando

Preface

The word *stress* hardly needs to be defined. (A quick Google search turned up more than four hundred million instances of the word on the Internet—yes, nearly half a billion!) I don't need to tell you what stress is. You already know about stress and stress disorders. People in every generation, the world over, know what it is firsthand. This of course includes this writer, who is an expert on stress from a standpoint of personal experience!

Some years ago I benefited from a program called the Stress Management Seminar put on by Dr. Henry Brandt, Dr. Sam L. Peeples, and Mary Glynn Peeples of Christian Ministries, Inc. in Birmingham, Alabama. They teach that stress is anything out of the ordinary that we have to adjust to (the external aspect) and the changes that occur in the body as it attempts to adjust (the internal aspect). The most important principle I carried away with me was that the stressful circumstance is not the key issue; it is the response that matters.[1]

Here is a unique quote from Drs. Brandt and Peeples:
The circumstances of life,
the events of life,
the people around me in life,
do not make me the way I am
but reveal the way I am.[2]

Personally, I don't like this quote. The reason I don't like it is if I agree with it, then I have to stop blaming everything else but myself and it's easier and more natural to blame everything and everybody but me.

Now, don't get your hopes up too high that this book is going to finally offer the cure for stress because a book that offers such ought not to be read, as it would be writing a check that could not be cashed.

I'm convinced that the only people without stress in

their lives are in heaven. Why? Because according to one of the millions of Web sites on stress, www.new-oceans.co.uk, stress is the price your body pays when life is not the way you'd like it to be.[3] It is my observation that most of us on Earth do not most of the time find life the way we'd like it to be. What the reading of this book and the application of its principles will promise, however, is that while there is no cure to completely eliminate stress, we can all learn to reduce stress and better learn to cope with stress. This book will help you do just that!

Acknowledgments

I wish to thank my elders (Eric Duncan, Jim Leonhard, Brian Overby, and Tom Pickens); my deacons (Chip Gregory, Bob Haley, Frank Liljeros, Tim Lockhart, Dale Pullis, and Tom Foley); my staff, who comfort me (Cheryl Gwinn, Daina Horner, Vicki Overby, and Susan Pullis); and all the River Oaks folks for their encouragement in allowing me this opportunity to try my hand at writing.

Thanks also to my new publishing family at Strang Communications and its publishing division Creation House, including Allen Quain and Jihan Ruano who initially reached out to this novice writer; and then Virginia Maxwell, who had the daunting task of walking me through this project; Atalie Andersen for her creative suggestions on the book's cover and copy; Amanda Lowell for dotting the Is and crossing the Ts; and last but not least, Robert Caggiano, for his editing expertise.

Introduction

Where we will start in this journey is in identifying the leading sources (some of which are unavoidable, some of which are avoidable) that cause and contribute to our stress. Once we have done so, we need to recognize the painful side effects of the damage our stress exacts on us and others around us. After we are in agreement as to the leading sources of our stress and the dangerous side effects, our journey will take us to some practical steps for reducing and coping with our stress.

Let the journey begin!
Meet the Stressmores

Meet Chris and Pat Stressmore and their two teenagers, a boy and a girl, plus their delightful but unplanned little addition, Johnny, who is now three. Chances are that you know this family. Monday through Friday, the drill is the same. (Unless one of the kids is sick and stays home from school. On such occasions, the best-laid plans come unraveled and the Stressmores are sent scrambling.) The teenagers are good kids, but after all, they are typical teenagers. In the mornings there never seems to be a right time to get into the bathroom, and the teenage daughter, once up, needs one of the two bathrooms all to herself. That leaves the other four of them to share the other bathroom if they don't get in and out of their daughter's before she needs it. Just getting them up is a chore, much less seeing that they comply with their parent's dress code, which the teenagers constantly remind them is stricter than the school's dress code or that of the local military school. Chris faintly remembers a slower pace in the mornings once upon a time that included everyone at the breakfast table starting their day with the day's "most important meal." There was also a time when Chris jogged every morning. Now, since the unplanned arrival and the kids turning into teenagers, all that is history—as is Chris's once-trim body.

If that were not hectic enough, it is becoming increasingly more difficult to keep everybody's weekday and weeknight schedule straight. To make things worse, scheduling falls to Chris simply because Chris is better at this type of thing than is Pat. As Chris reflects back to earlier, saner and simpler times, it seems now that they rarely eat together as a family as they once did. Only once and a while do they use their stove to cook a meal. Everybody seems to just eat fast food on the run.

Pat remembers when there was time spent with old college friends just hanging out. Their times together grew fewer and fewer as one got divorced, two moved away, and now Pat has no meaningful contact anymore with other females.

Weekends used to be more relaxed, a break from the maddening pace of life, something to which Chris and Pat used to look forward. Now sleeping late on Saturday is almost unheard of with all the sports and other activities the teenagers are involved in, activities that are now spilling over into Sundays as well. Sunday used to be a separate day of the week from all the others, but now Sundays seem just like any other day of the week. Both companies for which Chris and Pat work are working "meaner and leaner" these days, which translates into the occasional need for going into the office on Sundays.

Chris and the family used to go to church on a fairly consistent basis, but now if there is ever a time to sleep in or relax it is Sunday mornings. The family used to enjoy church and got a lot out of it, but they have gotten out of the habit. It has become easier and easier to not to go. At first they felt guilty, but that has worn off. If the teenagers don't go to church, Chris still insists that the kids go to youth group on Wednesday nights.

Besides all that, gas prices had gone up considerably, the cost of living is outstripping whatever raises they have received, and the cost of raising teenagers and a Johnny-come-lately is overwhelming. They considered getting a third car, but after pricing car insurance for a teenager that didn't seem to be a reality unless the teenagers got a job. If the kids got jobs, when would they ever be able to do homework and participate in all their youth activities—not to mention, When would they have time just to be kids? Both parents know that their kids will work all their adult lives and are in agreement that while they are being taught to be responsible and that they have their household chores, that work could be limited to summer jobs, which could help pay for their future college expenses. (That was their thought before summer school and church youth camps started entering the picture.)

Here again, once upon a time Chris followed a family budget, but that, too, is past history. Now both his body and budget are overweight. Today, Chris and family live hand to mouth, day by day, and for the most part having avoided the dreaded and inevitable emergency; they make ends meet fairly well. There was a time when they paid off their credit card each month and avoided the compound interest penalty from making the minimum monthly payment and rolling over their debt each month. But that was then and this is now. Now their credit card debt is mounting. This worries Chris, but he keeps this worry from Pat.

Last, but by no means least, Chris and Pat seem to be growing apart. Their whole life is devoted to their kids' lives. They have little or no time to themselves. Whatever intimacy they once enjoyed now seems forgotten. Chris and Pat can't remember when the two of them went to a movie or were alone together. They are simply too tired to work at their relationship. At one time they assured each other that their relationship would return when the kids were grown, but now they are not so confident. They wonder if they will be complete strangers by the time the kids are grown and move out of the house. Although neither would dare admit it to the other, both are for the first time starting to notice others at the office and seem to be aware of being noticed by others at the office. They independently convince themselves that a part of this is normal, that nothing will come of it, and yet for the first time it registers on their radar screens.

The teenagers are in different schools, which naturally have different schedules—and which further complicates school days. Fortunately they have worked out a carpooling arrangement for their older boy, but Chris has to take their daughter to school on the way to work. Pat's office is in the opposite direction but is on the way to Johnny's day care center. At least, these are the plans when it is not their week to carpool!

The Workaday World of Chris Stressmore

Now that you have been introduced to Chris, Pat, the teenagers, and their little surprise, we can get on with their story, which starts with Chris driving to the airport on this rainy Monday morning. Chris had to catch a nine o'clock roundtrip flight to Chicago to put out a fire that, if not put out, could have caused Chris's company to lose their biggest account. The stakes were huge. Chris was stressed by life in general and in particular by the thought of loosing that important customer, which accounted for more than 15 percent of their annual profits. Chris's plans called for him to be back home by midnight or catch a red eye in the morning so as to be able to take his daughter to school in the morning.

As luck would have it, traffic on the day of his departure was absolutely terrible. Even on a good day's traffic, driving to or from work in stop-and-go traffic was never Chris's favorite time of day. Going to the airport was even worse because the best route is right through downtown, the same route he used to get to work each day. Hardly a week went by without a fender-bender that brought traffic to a complete standstill, as the rubberneckers always slowed to check out the scene of the accident. Chris always got in the far left lane, the "fast lane," as soon as possible, and although the fast lane was full of the more aggressive and dangerous drivers, it seemed to move faster. The lanes to the right always seemed slower, as they have to make room for the merging traffic of the other, closer-in suburbanites merging on to the so-called expressway as they headed to their workaday worlds.

Chris got on his cell phone to check if his flight was leaving on time. This was one time when Chris hoped there would be a delay in the departure time. As he hit the speed dial, he looked to see if there were any police nearby, as it was illegal to make cell calls while driving. Chris learned the flight was scheduled to leave on time.

Chris turned the radio from the country western station to the traffic station and learned that there was an overturned semitrailer truck blocking the left and middle lanes. He decided to get over to the right in order to exit as soon as possible. Chris knew a shortcut that might save some time. He found that traffic was at a complete standstill. With both hands, he banged the steering wheel in utter frustration; accidentally, he hit the horn, which caused the driver of the car directly in front to display a particularly unkind finger gesture. At least the guy didn't come charging out of his car with a gun, exhibiting road rage, he thought.

While sitting there in traffic, Chris noticed a new billboard going up. The message on the billboard read:

Want to Stress Less?
www.stressless.com.

Chris noted the ironic play on his last name, made a mental note, and as soon as possible took the nearest exit for the shortcut on back roads to the airport. When Chris arrived near the airport, time was short and the airport parking lot Chris normally used was full.

To make a long story short, Chris missed the flight! He then called his client in Chicago to inform him that he would be late. Finally Chris caught a break, inasmuch as his client wanted to beg off the meeting anyway in order to get some additional figures together for their meeting. Chris gladly rescheduled the meeting for the next Monday with the assurances from the client that their relationship was still on solid ground.

Chris sat at the airport Gate 52 literally drained. It had already been a long day, and it was only 9:48 in the morning! Chris dutifully called the office to let them know of the change in plans and the good news that their client wasn't shopping around, at least not yet. Chris had another client, Dale, on that side of town and a personal visit would be in order especially since the client was once a close friend before life interfered with their relationship.

A Defining Moment for Chris Stressmore

Chris called and they set up a lunch appointment for 12:30 at Chili's. Chris arrived early and as he slid into the booth there was what looked like a credit card on the seat. Chris ordered a sweet tea and chips with queso. Upon inspection, it was not a credit card but a "Stressometer" produced by a company called WRS Group, Ltd., of Texas. Chris studied the card and followed the instructions. Not surprisingly Chris's stress level registered in the black, the highest level of stress: "tense"! Chris realized that this little measuring device did not represent state-of-the-art science, nor was it a substitute for a doctor's diagnosis, but it was nevertheless telling!

It was then the thought came to Chris about the billboard he saw just before exiting the expressway.

"What was the message on the billboard? What was the Web site? Something to do with stress," he tried to recall to himself. Chris googled the word *stress* and decided to glance through a few of the results. Here is the one that really grabbed Chris's attention:

Stress is the price your body pays when life is not the way you'd like it to be.
— www.newoceans.co.uk

The next was the real zinger for Chris. It triggered a

memory from way back, maybe one of his professors in college who said something that had stuck with him ever since:

Stress is like the common cold, which everybody seems to get, and for as long as it's been around, it's amazing that there is still no cure.

That one really started Chris to thinking! There was a truth to that statement that Chris didn't want to acknowledge, a truth that Chris would just as soon not face up to. This was a defining moment for Chris.

He was on the second bowl of chips when Dale squeezed into the opposite side of the booth. After some small talk they ordered, a peppercorn burger with fries for Chris and a guiltless chicken salad for Dale.

Dale noticed the Stressometer card on the table and inquired as to what it was. Chris explained that the person previously sitting there must have inadvertently left it. Chris said, "Here try it." Dale held the card between thumb and forefinger for fifteen seconds and registered in the blue, "calm." Chris felt even more stress at the moment, as inevitably the next thing his friend would ask was, "What did you register?" Chris's friend did not disappoint. Chris sheepishly answered, "Tense." Chris knew that would not be the end of the conversation and therefore spilled the beans nonstop over the next twenty minutes without even noticing the peppercorn burger and fries had arrived.

Now it was Dale's turn to speak. What Dale said was of great interest to Chris, who listened attentively.

Dale mentioned how similar life pressures or stress had led to a heart attack and a necessary number of changes in his lifestyle. Dale was kind enough not to point out that Chris was a leading candidate for a heart attack himself, but Chris knew without being told. As a matter of fact, recently, after feeling some tightness in the chest, Chris went to a doctor who could find nothing wrong with Chris. The physician chalked it up to stress.

A Lunch Napkin Worth Framing

Dale took a napkin and wrote in a vertical column the letters for *stress* like this:

S

T

R

E

S

S

Then Dale proceeded to explain how remembering what each of these letters stood for had initially helped him and how it became a constant source in helping him in to reduce the stress in his life.

Chris listened carefully, as what Dale had to say made sense. Chris asked Dale if he could keep the napkin as a reminder. Dale challenged Chris to come up with his own reminders using the six letters in the word *stress*.

Chris suddenly felt that this defining moment could easily slip away. He needed to ask Dale if he would meet with him on a regular basis for a while, for Dale to hold him accountable for following through on his good intentions to reevaluate his lifestyle to reduce stress. Dale quickly and willingly accepted the opportunity, as he himself had been lax of late in addressing the issue of stress in his own life.

Chris and Dale agreed to meet at Chili's again the following week after Chris got back from Chicago.

Chris headed back to the office excited about what the future held. He knew that things had to change or he was headed for a train wreck in almost every facet of his life. On the way back to the office Chris called Pat at work, which is something he only did in the case of an emergency. When Pat picked up the phone she was scared to death wondering what the emergency might be. Much to her relief, she found that there wasn't one and that Chris had not flown out to Chicago, nor had he lost his big client. Much to her surprise, she detected an excitement in Chris's voice that she had not heard for a long time.

Chris told Pat that the kids were home tonight, so he would pick up dinner for them and had asked the two older ones to sit for Johnny while they went out to dinner together. Pat was wondering what had gotten in to Chris when he told her he wanted them both to step back and take a serious look at their hectic lives and make some changes. Chris said that he would tell her all about what had come over him at dinner. Pat didn't know what to think but reservedly jumped at the invitation.

When Chris got to the office he attended to returning calls, visited the proper department to inform them of the postponement of today's meeting, and asked them to work up some additional figures and information in preparation for his meeting next week.

Chris then pulled out the napkin with Dale's handwriting. He reviewed what Dale had jotted down next to the six letters in the word stress.

Next to the first *s* Dale had written "spirituality." Then Chris recalled that Dale said that his choice of the order of the six letters were not necessarily in priority order, except this first one. Dale had said that as far as he was concerned, it drove all the others. The *t* stood for "time." The *r* for "relationships;" the *e* for "escape;" the second *s* for "spending;" and the last *s* for "shepherd."

While these principles were not exhaustive, they seemed to Chris to be pretty all-inclusive. He could think of a few substitutes, but thought that these would be hard on which to improve. Besides, Chris didn't want to get ahead of Pat. He wanted to get her on board and get her input so it could be "their" thing not just "his."

A Dinner Date with Pat

Chris left work and almost forgot to pick up the kids' dinner but didn't. The teenagers were not very pleased with Chris's choice of dinner, as he had stopped by Boston Market for something healthier than the kid's normal fare. "Boiled

Chicken?" their son said. Johnny wanted a Big Mac. Their daughter was having a hard time getting into her cheerleading outfit anyway and said she wasn't all that hungry. All of which their dad responded to by saying that there were going to be some upcoming changes in the eating habits of the Stressmore family.

Pat showered and changed outfits as though she were going on a date again. As they were walking out the door, Chris told her he had eaten at Chili's for lunch and asked her where she'd like to eat. Pat affectionately patted Chris's tummy and said that it looked like he had been eating there on a regular basis. Chris got defensive inside, but tried not to let it show. Pat realized she had hurt him and apologized asking what he had for lunch. Chris thought about the two bowls of chips with plenty of salt and queso and the grilled peppercorn burger and fries, but simply replied that he'd had a light lunch. Pat said that she, too, would like to eat something healthy for a change and suggested a new place that had just opened called The Garden, which featured a soup and salad bar. While Pat had not fought a weight problem, she was getting to the age where things started to go south physically speaking and she wanted to postpone the inevitable as long as possible.

The Garden was quiet and offered a nice table in the corner with candlelight. Chris couldn't remember the last time he ordered a bowl of soup and a Caesar salad, albeit one heavily sprinkled with croutons and Parmesan cheese. Pat had ordered potato soup with the house salad and light dressing.

Pat said, "Well, tell me about your day."

Chris responded by sharing some of the discoveries he had made regarding their family's lives in general and in particular about his personal revelations.

"In short," Chris continued, "I am stressed out in almost every area of my life."

This discovery came as no big shock to Pat.

Chris explained, "Look at all the stress we've been through in the last couple of years! First my father died. I've neglected my responsibility in the nurturing of our marriage relationship to the extent that I feel like we are strangers. Remember when we were scared to death when you discovered the lump on your breast, which, thank God, turned out negative? If that were not enough to break an elephant's back, everybody at the office is walking around the office on eggshells due to all the threats of layoffs because of the bad economy. I can't tell you the stress of wondering what would happen to us if I got laid off! Would we have to move? As it is, while we are keeping our heads above water, we are tighter financially than we've been since the early days of our marriage. If that weren't enough, need I remind you that Christmas is right around the corner and that if we are to treat Christmas normally, we will need to carry over our credit card debt? And finally, you have been very kind not to make a big deal of it, but I know that my mother coming to live with us is going to be a huge adjustment."

Time Out!

Let's temporarily leave the Stressmores while we discuss some of the leading causes of stress, many of which the Stressmores are experiencing.

Part I: Leading Stressors

Chapter 1

Personal Issues
I Want a Divorce

L inda and I have been married for forty-five years, many
of which have been stress filled! I can fully understand
why many couples get divorced. That is not an endorsement
for divorce, just a statement that recognizes that stress in
relationships is real and sometimes causes the undoing of
those relationships.

When one person lives on an island, they can do anything
they want. But it is a lonely existence. When another moves on
that same island, then neither of them can do exactly what they
want without causing stress to themselves and each other.

In my career, I have counseled many couples that were
going through the stresses of life together. Those that do not
learn to reduce or cope with stress either do not make it or
lived in a stress-filled prison of an unhealthy marriage.

Over the years I have been involved in the lives of several
couples that ended their relationship with a divorce. The
process of divorce only added to their stress, at least for the
long adjustment period following the divorce. Often the stress
they experienced in their first marriage is experienced again
in a subsequent marriage, especially as they entered a blended
marriage. I'm not speaking against blended marriages, just
merely relating the stress therein as reported to me by those in
such marriages. The most common problem I hear is the issue
of the children in each marriage not always accepting their
parent's new partner or getting along with the other children
brought into the merger.

The stress of the divorce process and subsequent
adjustments—lawyers, the financial cost, dividing of assets,

custody of the children, visitation rights, alimony, child support, the new life apart from one another, a new life alone of one party, or finding a new place to live—are enormous.

We're Bankrupt?

Money matters! Suffice it to say that spending is out of control in most of our lives.

ABC's *World News Tonight* ran a series titled "The Money Trap," in which they reported that Americans spent forty-two billion dollars more in 2005 than they made.[1] The report went on to say that Americans are saving less and living longer, which is a bad formula that does not bode well for their future.

There was an article in the July 24, 2006, *Orlando Sentinel* regarding a man who suffocated his wife and daughter, then killed himself. According to the story, the man and his wife were financial planners whose finances had gone bad (owed $113,127 in back taxes) and this was thought to be the motive behind the murders and suicide.[2] Granted, this is an extreme case, but it points out the ultimate extent to which some are driven by the financial stress in their lives.

We need to bring the money matters of our lives under control if we are going to have any hope of reducing the stress levels produced by undisciplined spending habits.

Wide Right Again?

Have you ever attended a Florida State-Florida football game? I personally rank the stress of a F.S.U. vs. Florida game just behind being fired from a job. You think that is bad? Some of my fellow alumni think it's way ahead of death on the stress charts.

For more years than I'd like to recall, F.S.U. lost critical games—I mean with the national championship on the line—when a field goal went inexplicably and errantly off to the right. Even if F.S.U. wins, it is stressful, but at least F.S.U. supporters have bragging rights for an entire year. But how does one deal with the stress of seeing his or her alma mater lose against its number one interstate rival?

While I don't rank an F.S.U. loss above death, a loss in late November can come near to ruining Christmas.

Chapter 2

Health Issues
You Have Tested Positive

"You tested positive for cancer" are words we dread and hope never to hear from our doctor. A close second stressor to hearing these words are the long, agonizing days leading up to hearing these words after one has had a biopsy and the days after surgery wondering if the other shoe is going to drop. With every little twinge or ache or pain, one wonders if it has come back. Not to mention the indignities and rigors of chemo and radiation, the hair loss, the disfigurement, the colostomy, reconstruction surgery, and other horrible side effects.

I've had the privilege of walking through the process with more people than I can remember. I say *privilege* because those with whom I walked as a pastor have been very brave and have ministered to me with their fortitude and courage far more than I have ministered to them.

I'll never forget the day as a youngster when I read that Joseph Salk discovered the cure for polio, the cancer-like scare of my childhood memory. I welcome the day when we read together of a cure for cancer, AIDS, MS, diabetes, and other diseases that ravage our loved ones' and friends' bodies.

Other Stressors

Now that we've described some of the leading causes of stress and before we rejoin the Stressmores for dinner, let's take a brief look at the toll that stress has on our minds, bodies, and spirits.

Chapter 3

Life Issues
Better Call the Family

My dad's death was traumatic for me. I was one of the fortunate ones to have had an absolutely super dad. His death at seventy-six seemed too early and we were robbed of too much life together, too many rounds of golf, and hanging out.

Mom called several times that year to tell me Dad had gone into the hospital, but he always came out. Mom called once again, only that time to say the doctor's didn't think he would make it. I stood by his bedside for several stress-filled days, day and night watching my seemingly invincible hero die, very much to my dismay.

In my profession I am constantly involved with the death of others' loved ones. Probably the worst—if the stress of death can be ranked—is the death of a child. Certainly the death of a spouse is terrible, even more so than what I experienced with my dad, but the death of a child seems the most stressful of all, as it just isn't expected for a parent to outlive their child. It is stressful on the surviving siblings as well.

I can only imagine what it must be like. I have a faint idea, inasmuch as our daughter nearly died of spinal meningitis at the age of three. That experience is to this day, thirty-eight years later, as vivid as any among the stressful experiences of my life. For what seemed like an eternity, we didn't know if Ann would live or die, or if she lived, whether she would suffer any brain damage. Fortunately, she came through with no problems other than two stressed out but grateful parents.

My first ministry experience with the death of a child was in Minneapolis. The police called to inform me that the daughter (a young woman in her early twenties) of a couple in the church had died in an automobile accident. The police asked if I would go to the house that Sunday morning to inform them, and I did. The resulting stress registered in them and me was predictably palpable.

My next experience was in Atlanta. I was called out of a meeting with the officers of the church to take an emergency phone call from the girlfriend of a young college student. She tearfully related to me that her boyfriend, a member of our church, had tragically died in a freak accident in which he was trapped in a truck and burned to death. I broke the news to his parents and spent the rest of the night with them in their shock and sadness. Not long after, his father left his mother. I wonder to this day how much the stress of his son's death had to do with his leaving.

Another stressful time was when one of the young mothers in my church was in an automobile accident in which her unborn baby died after she hit the steering wheel of her car. The graveside service and littlest casket I've ever seen were sad and stressful to say the least.

A friend of ours lost her unborn baby at approximately eight months, but it was recommended that she carry her baby to term and give birth. In my pastoral experience, that was far and away the most stress-filled birth ever. The starkness of the contrast was amazing and terrible. Instead of phoning family and friends and all the ooh-ing and ah-ing and passing out of cigars it was a tragic day.

Miscarriages are another example among the stressful experiences of life. Once I actually had an expectant mother miscarry her baby while visiting in my office. Sadder still was that it was a high-risk pregnancy and the last pregnancy this childless woman would ever experience.

One of my wife's best friends lost a young son to cancer. As strong in faith as she and her husband are, that event stands out as the source of the most stressful pain in their lives.

My wife's mother died in early 2008 at the ripe old age of ninety-three. Her sister and brother took turns going down to visit her in their many stressful visits. Even though her death was anticipated for some time, we all became acquainted with the stressful aftermath of activities and responsibilities common in the concluding of one's estate. If you haven't been through this there is little you can do to prepare yourself for the stress, but what little you can do (setting up a trust; obtaining a power of attorney; executing wills and livings wills; knowing your loved one's wishes for the funeral service; prearranging for the disposal of their estate) you ought to do before it is too late. This will take a lot of the stress of the event off your shoulders later when death becomes the reality.

I asked a lady leaving church one Sunday how she was handling the death of her mother, and she indicated that she had been doing well until her mother's birthday; and then the bottom fell out once again. Thanksgiving and Christmas would not be any easier, either, for a while at least—if ever—nor will certain special places or flowers or food or anything else that serves as a reminder of what has been lost.

Suicides are another stress-related tragedy. No telling the amount of stress that it takes for one to resort to such a terrible end of life, not to mention the stress that this places on those they leave behind. I've experienced a few cases in my ministry in which there was an unsuccessful suicide attempt, along with a few that were successful. The buildup of stress in the person's life and the feelings of hopelessness that lead to suicide certainly must be horrible.

One other occurrence is murder, some of which are no doubt related to stress in some part. I recall one couple I met early on in my present ministry. They separated after many bouts of anger, throwing things, biting, and scratching, mostly attributed to alcohol. I will never forget the day I received a phone call that came subsequent to their separation informing me that the husband had entered the home his wife was still living in, shot and killed her and her lover, and then turned the gun on himself. None survived except the wife's teenage son, who was in the home asleep at the time. The son went to live with his father in another state, and I've not heard from him since.

We better learn to deal with the stress brought on by death because sooner or later we will all experience it in one way or another.

You're Fired

If you have ever watched the television show *The Apprentice*, then you have heard Donald Trump say these words as he pointed his finger at the person or persons who are getting disqualified from the supposed honor of being hired into the Trump organization. Unfortunately for some, the matter of being fired is not just a TV show in which those fired had never had the job to begin with but a reality of life in the corporate world.

Soften it as we might to "being let go" or "being downsized" or "resigning" (often a euphemism for being forced to resign), it still is the beginning of one of the most stressful times in a person's life. If they have a family, it is compounded!

One of my friends moved just outside of Charlotte, North Carolina. All was well for the first few months until out of the blue it appeared he fell victim to company politics and was betrayed by a man he looked up to, who in order to save his own neck, left my friend to hang out to dry. My friend's reputation was unfairly besmirched and in the close corporate community in which he traveled, it has hurt him in the subsequent job search process. It was a long, stressful year before he landed a job.

Presently, there is a man in our church who was let go. While he is a prince of a guy, whip-smart with the computer, and would be an asset to any company, he is cursed with being in his fifties. His initial efforts to get another job have not proved fruitful thus far, and he and his family are about to reach the difficult place of eating into savings, retirement funds, and their home equity. All of these were to be designated for retirement. If that weren't bad enough, speaking as a man for men, our egos are the most damaged of all. I'm the old-fashioned provider type and so is he, so I can imagine what he is going through. Adding to the stress of his situation is the possibility that he may need to consider moving to another state where there are job openings in his area of expertise.

The Hurricane Is a Category 4!

Have you ever lived through two hurricanes within a couple of months? On behalf of my wife, Linda, and dog, Caleb, I nominate hurricanes just behind the death of a loved one. Caleb gets so hyper-stressed out when he hears thunder and lightning that he shakes uncontrollably and is utterly inconsolable. His doctor, Jim Califf, who makes house calls, recommended Xanax, but that hasn't helped Caleb. His best coping mechanism is to go into the half bath downstairs with the light and fan on, but alas during a hurricane we are usually without electricity for days! What's worse, Linda makes Caleb appear calm! I hope you think that is funny because I am going to pay for that one. By order of Linda, we are not allowed to sleep upstairs in our beds but must sleep downstairs, preferably in the stairs closet. Even if I laid aside my Scottish heritage and purchased a gas generator, hurricanes would still be high on the list of stressors.

Coincidentally, it has just started to thunder and lightning (this is a frequent occurrence in Central Florida—a.k.a. The Lightning Capital of the world—especially in the summer months, and from the guest bedroom (the appointed work station of this would-be writer) I can hear the unmistakable squealing noises—cries, if you will—that Caleb makes from his throat when he is scared and the clicking of his toenails on the tile floor downstairs as he goes into his frantic little dance. Caleb makes no bones that this is the number one stressor in his life.

The Katrina victims could laugh at the stress we suffered at the hands of Charley and Frances.

We're Moving Again?

I remember in my former life (no, I do not believe in

reincarnation; I am referring to my life as a banker, but if reincarnation were true, I'd like to come back as a successful writer the next time around) that IBM stood for "I've been moved" and GE stood for "gone elsewhere."

The last statistic I heard on the subject was that the average mortgage in America lasted four years! I realize that this could be attributed, in large part, due to refinancing. Still, we Americans move a lot, and it's usually not next-door.

If you start with my banking career, we have moved to Atlanta from Coral Gables; from Coral Gables back to Atlanta; from Atlanta back to Coral Gables again; from Coral Gables to the Boston area; from the Boston area to Minneapolis; from Minneapolis to Atlanta; and from Atlanta to Lake Mary, Florida. Counting them, that is six moves in forty-five years, an average of moving every seven years, not taking into account that we moved six times in Atlanta from one house to another, nor that we have been in the same place for the past seventeen years!

I recently moved my mother, at her request, into a retirement home in North Carolina. She was eighty-five at the time. According to her, just about everything was damaged or missing. I filled out the claim form but was told by the moving company that we were supposed to have checked each item against the bingo sheet as it came off the truck! Puh-leese! After contacting my local newspaper's troubleshooter/consumer advocate extraordinaire, I eventually had a resolution, which included a settlement of a whopping one thousand dollars.

I've never met anybody who liked moving except the moving companies, and to look at the expression on the faces of the drivers and their pick-up labor, they don't seem to like it either. There is the stress of packing; the timing of when the movers come; and when they arrive at your new location (which never has worked smoothly for us), getting reimbursed from the moving company for damage claims; the unpacking; meeting new people; finding a new place to get a hair cut, beauty parlor, grocery store, where to get the car fixed, good places to eat, doctors and dentists; a new mortgage; new driver's license;

license plates; opening a new bank account—you know the drill. Need I go on?

Only Thirty More Shopping Days 'Til Christmas

The holidays (derived from the term *holy days*) can be anything but holy, peaceful, and restful but can be and often are chock full of stress!

Have you ever heard of the holiday blues?

Take Christmas for example. This is supposed to be the season to be jolly and merry, right? Everybody is supposed to be "Ho! Ho! Ho!" but instead it's "go, go, go"—traffic, long shopping lines, stressed-out store clerks, spending more than we have to spend by charging what we will pay dearly for later.

Christmas has become anything but a time of peace on Earth.

In his book, *Cold Moon*, author Jeffery Deaver's characters are conversing on Christmas when the character "Sellitto sang, 'Tis the season to be killing...' Pulaski gave a frown. Rhyme explained to him, 'The deadliest times of the year are hot spells and holidays. Remember, Ron: Stress doesn't kill people, people kill people—but stress makes them do it.'"[1]

There are more suicides at Christmas than at any other time of the year.

Depression is at an all-time high at Christmas. What can add to this depression is the already mentioned going through the holidays without a loved one who helped make these days special.

Have I mentioned yet the stress of family coming to visit or us going to visit family? If that isn't enough, how about the endless number of parties (office, church, other)?

Christmas has gotten out of hand.

If Christmas has gotten out of hand, how about weddings? I know these are not holidays, but they are huge stressors. According to a report ABC *World News Tonight* in 2006, the average cost of a wedding in the US is $28,000![2] And how about birthdays? Anniversaries? Mother's Day? Father's Day?

Holidays should be something to which we look forward, but about all that they produce is stress. Do I sound like Scrooge?

Part II: Leading Symptoms

Chapter 4

Mind

MacDonald Consultants list some of the mental symptoms of stress as:[1]
Forgetfulness
Low productivity
Negative attitude
Lethargy
No new ideas
Poor concentration

As opposed to:
Creative flow
Positive attitude
Growth through learning
When my mind goes on overload, I sense a weariness in my ability to think properly. My mind goes to mush. One vacation several years ago, Linda and I rented a condo at the beach. Linda was upset with me the first day that I didn't want to come out and play. I kept telling her that I wasn't ready yet. I was in such a bad state of mind going into the vacation that it took me three days to recover before I wanted to go out and play.

Since I've never attempted to write before, I'm in a whole new paradigm of the mind. I don't know what writers experience. I find I'm good for a couple of hours at a sitting, and I am not good for more than a couple sittings a day. This is tedious and taxing work. Yesterday was the Fourth of July and the first day I have completely taken off since I started eight days ago. Yesterday I was a bit stressed-out thinking I was being lazy. Today I was eager to get back at it again and feel fresher. There is a lesson on dealing with stress there somewhere. Hang on to that thought until the sections on time (the Sabbath Principle) and escape.

Chapter 5

Body

Macdonald Consulting lists some of the following as physical symptoms of stress:[1]
Appetite/weight change
Insomnia
Muscle aches
Digestive upsets
Teeth grinding
Addictions

As opposed to:
Feeling up/energetic
Strength/stamina
Feeling "on"

A compilation of medical sources is constantly pointing their finger at stress as a factor in causing illnesses like cancer. Stress causes changes in the immune system—the body's line of defense against disease. Stress interferes with the body's ability to fight off tumor cells and other virus-infected cells in the body. Stress decreases the ability of natural killer cells to recognize and kill infected virus cells.

Brandt and Peeples inform us that people who do not deal well with stress will have lower natural killer cells or white blood cells (the foot soldiers of the body's immune system) than those who deal well with stress.[2]

Twenty-five years ago, the June 6, 1983, issue of *Time* magazine carried an article stating that in addition to cancer, stress is a contributor to coronary heart disease, lung ailments, accidental injuries, cirrhosis of the liver, suicide, multiple

17

sclerosis, diabetes, genital herpes, and trench mouth.[3] In this article, the American Academy of Physicians claimed that two-thirds of all office visits were in some way prompted by stress. I cite this dated source to show that stress has been on our radar for a long time and yet to the detriment of our health, we seem to be making little progress in reducing and coping with it.

The absolute worst physical response I've ever had to stress came when I left banking to take over the family building supply business. The physical stress symptom was diarrhea, which stemmed primarily from my huge desire to please my father, as well as some secondary factors.

I lived on Lomotil, a prescription drug that fights diarrhea, for the whole year I worked for Dad. There was never a moment when I wasn't checking where the bathrooms were in case I needed one, and I needed one often. If you live this way, you have my deepest understanding.

Strike one: Little did I know when I came into the business that we would share an office—a small office—in which our desks faced one another. Dad had all this business experience, which was guided by tremendous business instincts. I've never known anyone like him. He just instinctively knew when to get in and out of a business deal, when to buy and when to sell. He was not college-educated. He was a man of the old school, a man who brought himself up by his bootstraps.

On the other hand I was a novice to the building supply business but eager to learn. There was a warehouse full of materials of which I needed to learn the names and uses. I was unacquainted with the suppliers, purchasing, and our customers. Dad had an old hand accounting system that was antiquated and too slow to keep pace with the times. I had just come from the largest bank in the southeast and was accustomed to the latest in computer-backed and other backup systems.

But I knew I could sell, or at least I thought I knew!

Strike two: First of all, Dad went into the building supply business from the roofing business. His idea was that he could make a good living selling to all the roofers he had known and competed against for years. Furthermore, Dad had good credit standing with the roofing suppliers, so it seemed a natural. The vision was that the sale of roofing supplies could pay the bills until we got the contractor's supply end of the business up and running.

It turns out that there was a well-established competitor in the contractor's supply end who bought product by the train car loads, and all we could afford to do was to buy by the truck load. It didn't take me long to figure out we were at a big price disadvantage from the get-go.

Strike three: Dad had sold his roofing business to a young man he had brought up in the business. The reality was that Dad had nothing to do with the roofing business anymore. It didn't take this sales hot shot long to find out that there is a huge difference between reality and perception! As I would go to Dad's former competitors to sell them roofing products, I got a cool reception as their perception was that dad was a silent partner in the old roofing business and that he would sell to the old roofing business at lower prices, which would put it at an advantage in the bidding process. I wasn't a good enough salesman to convince them otherwise.

If that wasn't bad enough, I found the contractor's supply end of the business to be cutthroat. I'd walk into a construction trailer with my price list in hand but was largely ignored by the job supers, many of whose attention was gained not by better prices (we'd sometimes undercut our competitor's price in order to gain a foot in the door) and better service but by a small "gift" of some sort, frequently taking the form of football tickets. Dad and I agreed we wouldn't play that game.

To make a long story short, Dad had a very capable man running things for us in our Broward County office, where many of these negative dynamics were not present. Because we were operating in the red in Dade County and in the black in Broward County, we made the only decision we could—concentrate in Broward County and service what few profitable accounts we had in Dade out of the Broward office.

Eventually I left the family business and went to seminary, the business was subsequently sold, and the minute I left, so did the diarrhea.

Chapter 6

Spirit

According to MacDonald Consulting, these are some of the spiritual symptoms of stress:[1]
Restlessness
Emptiness/doubt
Unforgiving
Martyrdom
Loss of direction
Cynicism/apathy

As opposed to:
Peace/joy
Purpose
Order/coherence
Optimism

I have experienced a stressful spirit in different ways in each of the three churches I have had the privilege of serving as pastor. We have all experienced the stressful first day on the job. In Minneapolis I recall sitting in my office on the first day and asking myself the question, What do I do? I'd never been a pastor before. It was my first day and I didn't know exactly what to do. I didn't remember having a seminary course on what to do the first day. But that soon went away as I became immersed in ministry. I was like a kid with a new toy. I jumped at any and every opportunity to serve. I loved every minute of it, but it wasn't long before it caught up with me.

I want to point out that the depletion of my spirit was not the church's fault, but mine. Somehow I naively thought that you could work eighty to ninety hours a week and the Lord would give you the energy necessary to do His work! Not so. I learned the hard way that I needed to work smarter, not longer.

In the meantime, however, my spirit was being starved by giving out so much and not taking in. In his book *The Friendless American Male*, David W. Smith likens this state of spirit unto being a vending machine of which others have been pulling on your levers and you are all out of stock, empty, depleted with nothing left to give.[2] I learned that the demands of serving need to be met by supplying yourself with times of feeding your own spirit. As I read the Scriptures, I realized that even Jesus got away from the maddening crowd to pray and spend time with His Father. If Jesus needed to recharge His spiritual batteries, then what does that say about you and me?

In Atlanta I experienced the depletion of my spirit in another way. I took over a church in transition from a much-revered long-serving pastor to a church without him. There had actually been two other pastors in between him and me, but his shadow was still cast over the church in a way that made it difficult for anyone after him to be effective. When I broke with some of the style and traditions of the former pastor, the proverbial doo-doo hit the fan. In its own way, the first several years there were the hardest in my thirty-plus years in the ministry. I still have scars in my spirit from those early years in Atlanta. Fortunately, the hard years did not last and better years followed, which helped end my service there on a positive note.

As I was nearing the age of fifty, I had a sense that the Lord was calling me to start a new church. Lake Mary, Florida, ended up being the place. Starting a church from scratch in a place I'd never heard of was a different level of the stress of the spirit than I had ever faced. There were no big bands playing as I entered the city, no one knew I was coming and furthermore, no one cared. Where will we meet? How will we make it financially? (We were given eighteen months to be self supporting or else.) Will anybody come to our first worship service? These were questions I had never had to deal with before. This was a bigger step of faith than Minneapolis or Atlanta. The stakes were higher, the risk was huge, the possibility for failure real. All of this took its toll on my spirit.

Once we got off the ground (did you hear the story of the pastor who used to go to park near the airport runway to see something get off the ground without his help?) there were staff issues, people being transferred away, people who left to go to another local area church, one thing after another.

Before stress takes its toll on our minds, bodies, and spirits, we better get a handle on how to deal with it. We who are battered about in mind, body, and spirit by stress need, "The Touch of the Master's Hand":[3]

Well, it was battered and scarred,
And the auctioneer felt
It was hardly worth his while
To waste much time on the old violin,
But he held it up with a smile.
"It sure ain't much
But it's all we got left.
I guess we ought to sell it too.
Oh, now who'll start the bid
On this old violin?
Just one more and we'll be through."
And then he cried,
"One, give me one dollar.
Who'll make it two?
Only two dollars?
Who'll make it three?
Three dollars twice now,
That's a good price,
Now who's got a bid for me?
Raise up your hand now,
Don't wait any longer,
The auction's about to end.

Who's got four?
Just one dollar more,
To bid on this old violin?"
Well, the air was hot,
And the people stood around
As the sun was settin' low.
From the back of the crowd,
A gray-haired man
Came forward and picked up the bow.
He wiped the dust
From the old violin,
Then he tightened up the strings,
And then he played out a melody
Pure and sweet,
Sweet as the angels sing.
And when the music stopped,
The auctioneer, with a voice
That was quiet and low,
He said, "Now what am I
Bid for this old violin?"
Then he held it up with the bow.
And then he cried out,
"One, give me one thousand?
Who'll make it two?
Only two thousand?
Who'll make it three?
Three thousand twice,
You know that's a good price,
Come on who's got a bid for me?"
And the people cried out,
"What made the change?
We don't understand."
Then the auctioneer stopped
And he said with a smile,
"It was the touch of the master's hand."

You know there's many a man
With his life out of tune,
Battered and scarred with sin.
And he's auctioned cheap
To a thankless world,
Much like that old violin.
Then the Master comes,
And the foolish crowd,
They never understand,
Oh, the worth of a soul,
And the change that's wrought
Just by one touch of the Master's hand.

* * * *

Meanwhile, Back to the Stressmores...

Now let's rejoin the Stressmores for dinner, where we pick up with Chris just having dumped a huge load on Pat in the way of a truthful and painful confession regarding his revelation of the stress in his (their) lives.

Chris then showed Pat the Stressometer. Pat registered orange, which represents "some tension."

Seeing the look on Pat's face and realizing that she was trying her best to assimilate the tremendous weight of what he had told her (I believe the term is *TMI* for "too much information"), Chris quickly shifted gears to share the good news of what he proposed to stress less. With that, he pulled out the now-crumpled napkin to show Pat the acronym for *stress* that Dale had shown him at lunch.

Pat agreed that an application of the six words from the acronym would definitely lead to less stress *if* applied properly and regularly. Pat was concerned however, that this could be more easily shared than implemented.

Chris agreed and suggested that they each take some time individually to think about this and that they would have dinner again in a week, at which time they would discuss this in greater detail.

The next dinner date proved frustrating, as each admitted to the other that they had indeed put some thought into the six words of the acronym, but that they hadn't made much progress as to how to move forward in an effort to effectively stress less.

* * * *

Maybe you can identify with the Stressmores in many ways, i.e. you acknowledge that your life is stressful; you would like to take action to stress less; you are intrigued with the acronym for stress, but you are not quite sure how to apply these principles to your life.

Let me jumpstart the process by helping you with some more in-depth ideas for each of the six words. (You are also intelligent enough and totally free to attach your own words to each of the six letters of *stress*.)

The following are the words that help me reduce and cope with stress by pointing to the various means of learning to reduce and cope with stress. I hope they will prove helpful to you as well.

Spirituality
Time
Relationships
Escape
Spending
Shepherd

Part III: Leading Stress Solutions

Chapter 7

S Is for Spirituality

It seems natural coming off a discussion of spirit that it is appropriate to discuss spirituality.

According to the first question of *The Larger Catechism of the Westminster Confession of Faith*, the main purpose of our existence is to glorify God and enjoy Him forever, yet...

We worship our work.

We work at our play.

We play at our worship.

As my mother used to say, we have it all backwards.

We constantly care for and feed our minds and our bodies while we neglect our spirits, which go largely uncared for and as a result are starved. Little wonder we are so filled with stress. In my opinion, this is the root cause of all stress.

Do you realize what a huge statement I just made? I just said that the root cause of stress is a neglect of the spirit, for I believe if the spirit is right with God, then stress is eliminated. Now I know I have previously said that there is no complete cure for stress. Am I contradicting myself? No. Why not? Because the spirit is never permanently right with God this side of heaven. That fact shouldn't keep us from trying, however. That act of trying is a part of what it means to worship. The other part, the bigger part, is trusting.

Unless or until we properly practice a lifestyle of worship, we will fail in our efforts to reduce and cope effectively with stress.

I paraphrase Blasé Pascal, the French philosopher who said that there is a vacuum in every person's heart, a place that God alone can fill. We all sense that void and naturally attempt to fill that sacred place with things other than God (good books, food, alcohol, drugs, sex, fame, wealth, cars, jewelry, an F.S.U. victory over Florida; you name it), and while these can provide a temporary fix, we eventually come up empty and wanting.

Man, male and female, is created in the image and likeness of our Creator. What does it mean to be created in His image and likeness? As spiritual beings, created in His likeness and image, we are to spiritually resemble Him. He is the sum total of all of His divine perfections or attributes. He is omniscient (all-knowing), omnipresent (all or everywhere present), and omnipotent (all-powerful), and in these ways we can but worship Him and stand in awe of Him. There is no way for us to copy these attributes of God. He neither expects nor wants us to try to copy Him in these ways. These are just a few examples that set Him apart as God.

There are other attributes that, while we nonetheless still worship Him for perfectly possessing, He desires for us to copy. They are attributes like love, joy, peace, patience, kindness, goodness, faithfulness, gentleness, and self-control, to name a few.

The bad news is that until we have entered into a personal relationship with Him, try as we might, we will fail in our attempts to shadow our Creator. Some reading this might be surprised that God desires a personal relationship with us. The truth is that He far more desires a personal relationship with us than we do with Him. The key to entering into that relationship is the trusting part, and prior to that, the trying part is fruitless.

Here again, we have things all backwards. We have it in our thick hearts that we must win God's favor by trying. This is a major factor in producing stress. The good news is that we already have God's favor. That's where the trust part comes in. Again, this is the ultimate way to reduce stress.

And it—*trust*—needs to come first!

Chapter 8

T Is for Time

A ll of our time comes from Him.
How do you spend the time He gives you?

So many of us are living in the fast lane, traveling at mach speed with our hair on fire.

Gordon MacDonald in his classic book *Ordering Your Private World*, reminds us of the three laws of time: time is inelastic, the truth here being that there are only twenty-four hours in every day available to us, no matter who we are.[1] Next, time is indispensable. Everything requires time. And last, time is irreplaceable. There isn't anything you can substitute for time. While I don't think we think consciously of these laws all the time, subconsciously they are always there driving the deadlines set by us or others.

One of the gems of a lifetime was written by Charles Hummel in his book *The Tyranny of the Urgent*, wherein he warned of being so focused on the urgent business at hand that we forget the important.[2] Are you failing to do the important because of the constant urgency of the urgent? Another Hummel gem is: beware of the barrenness of a busy life.[3] Is your life threadbare from traveling the fast lane of life? Is it time to pull into pit road for a tire change?

After all these years of life, I have come to agree with Gordon MacDonald that those who are driven experience a much greater sense of stress in their lives than those who are called. Beware, type-A personalities.

MacDonald points this out using my favorite movie, *Chariots of Fire*. Do yourself a favor and rent this movie for your viewing pleasure and inspiration. This movie, which came out in the early eighties, depicts two men, Harold Abrams of

England and Eric Liddle of Scotland (nicknamed "the Flying Scot"). Each man was a gifted runner with world-class speed. Abrams was the picture of the driven man. Winning was all that mattered, all he lived for. Liddle, on the other hand, although no less passionate or focused, was a man who knew he was called by God. At this part of his life he was called to run and felt God's pleasure when he did so.

The movie portrays each in their separate countries as they trained until finally they met head to head. Liddle won. Abrams was devastated. As the story unfolds and as we are led to its climax, both Abrams and Liddle are chosen to represent Great Britain in the 1924 Olympics in Paris.

The one thing that is obvious to me about the characters in the movie, in my personal experience, and in my experience with others is this: the called ones lead less stress-filled lives than the driven ones.

The question arising from this movie is, Are you a driven or called man or woman? Take a look at your priorities. When I ask men and women what their priorities are, the standard answer—if they have thought in those terms—goes something like this: family, work, and others. Some even place God somewhere in the equation of life.

The acid test comes when I ask them to do an exercise for me by filling out a typical week's schedule as to how they spend their time. I do this because nothing reflects one's priorities as does the time one spends on them.

The following is a simple form on which you can chart your typical week.

	SUNDAY	MONDAY	TUESDAY	WEDNESDAY	THURSDAY	FRIDAY	SATURDAY
5:00							
6:00							
7:00							
8:00							
9:00							
10:00							
11:00							
12:00							
1:00							
2:00							
3:00							
4:00							
5:00							
6:00							
7:00							
8:00							
9:00							
10:00							
11:00							

What has been helpful to me is to divide each day into three segments or sections: morning (from the time I get up to noon); afternoon (noon to dinner time); and evening (dinner time to bedtime). That leaves a fourth segment for sleep. Just as we should budget our money, so too should we budget our time.

That would make three awake segments, of which there are seven each week, for a total of twenty-one awake segments and one sleep segment each day, times seven for a total of seven sleep segments.

First, let's concentrate on the twenty-one segments per week in which we are awake.

Everyone has different energy levels based on factors like health and age, so not everybody can effectively utilize as many awakened segments as everybody else.

In addition, there are rhythms to each our lives. Some of us are morning people and some of us night owls. If you are a night owl, then ending the third segment at 11:00 p.m. is as ridiculous to you as getting up at 5:00 a.m., just as going to bed after nine or 10:00 p.m. is ridiculous to me since I get up at 5:00 a.m. most days. Plus, there are seasons of life. A person with young children will have a different-looking schedule than empty nesters or those without children.

All these factors need be taken into account to make the most effective use of the twenty-one awake segments.

Still with me?

Ok, so it is up to each of us to recognize our own individual energy levels, rhythms, the times of day we are most energetic, and our particular seasons of life as we analyze how we utilize the twenty-one awake segments available to us in a typical week.

For me, I am good for about twelve to fifteen segments of work each week. Any less than that and I would have to look for another calling; any more than that and I am completely stressed out.

Furthermore, my mind, body, and spirit tell me that I am not capable of productively working twelve to fifteen straight back-to-back segments (even allowing for sleep segments in between). Therefore, because I tend to be a morning person, I schedule the brain-energy work (e.g., sermon research preparation) on the morning segments; and other job activities (e.g., hospital calls and routine administrative work) for the afternoon segments.

My second most important priority (I will reveal my number one priority later) is spending time with my family (Linda first, children second). Therefore, one of my goals is to spend at least four nights a week at home. In addition, my calling is a bit different than your normal workaday world in which one typically works Monday through Friday and has the weekends off. In my calling, I typically work Monday through Thursday, take Fridays off, work at least one Saturday and Sunday segment, usually three or four. So if I work Monday through Thursday, that's eight segments; I'm usually out two to three nights a week, which is another two or three segments (we are now up to a total of ten to eleven segments), and then add weekends, another two to four, and I am at twelve to fifteen.

Now back to the initial point of the exercise, comparing one's priorities to one's schedule.

Chart a typical week's schedule and see how your priorities are reflected in your schedule. In my experience in doing this with people, nine out of ten times it isn't! The logical thing to do is either to rearrange your priorities or rearrange your schedule or a combination of the two. If your priorities are straight, then a rearranging of your schedule is in order to reflect your priorities.

It may sound contradictory for me to list my family as my number two priority and yet not spend as much time with them as I do working or sleeping. This need not be contradictory, as my family is understanding enough and know that I will spend more time working and sleeping than I will with them. The key to them being the true higher priority than work or sleep lies in the quality of time I spend with them.

Two other applications related to time that will reduce

your stress or help you to better cope with it are sleep and what I call the Sabbath Principle.

Regarding the sleep segment, we all recognize that we do not all require the exact same amount of sleep. However, most sane and sober individuals would acknowledge that we all require somewhere between six and ten hours of sleep. Let's bring it to the norm of which most speak, and that is eight hours. I have found out the hard way that I need between seven and eight hours myself.

I once read that tired football players injure the easiest. I know for a personal fact that when I am deprived of my seven to eight hours I injure more easily, am less productive, more irritable, and generally no fun to be around.

How much sleep do you require? (Honestly now, no blowing smoke.) Are you regularly getting it? If not, my conclusion is that, all things being equal, you will have more stress than those who do get their required amount of sleep.

What I call the Sabbath Principle is not original with me, but actually was first put into effect by our Creator. Remember that He made all that He made in a span of six days, and then even God rested. In doing so, He who made us and knows us better than we know ourselves recognized that a part of the rhythm and pattern of life is to work six days and rest one.

Again, the people I know that religiously follow this God-given rhythm are less stressed-out than those who constantly violate it. Regardless of if one follows this practice out of biblical or Christian convictions, even those who do so for other reasons will reduce their stress and find a greater ability to cope with stress.

Are you regularly working seven days a week? Some say to me in using an excuse allowed for in the Bible that their ox is constantly in the ditch. My comeback is, either kill the ox or fill in the ditch!

Let me share with you a true story that illustrates God's point. During World War II, the Parker Boat Company in Orlando, Florida, was commissioned by the government to make amphibious landing boats used for transporting soldiers from onboard ship to the beach for landings. As the demand increased and because Parker was making a good product, their orders increased as well. Initially, Parker had to go to two shifts, and as the government orders increased, they went to three. Get this: Parker could not make in seven days of three shifts what they could make in six days of three shifts! Amazing? Not really. They proved God's point. Just as there are physical laws that govern the universe, like the law of gravity, there are also spiritual laws. Among the many seemingly strange and mysterious spiritual laws is that one cannot consistently do in seven days what one can do in six. Go figure!

What about you? Are you observing one day in seven to rest from the other good things He has given you to do the other six? If not, you will pay for it by adding unnecessary stress to your life.

Stress is also greatly reduced by the touch of the Master's hand through healthy relationships.

Chapter 9

R Is for Relationships

A popular speaker I once heard said that five years from now the books you read and the people you meet will have made the greatest difference in your life. However, I know that one of my personal obstacles in making friends is that I am naturally wired as an introvert. I like people, but I don't feel I need people. This is harmful, because God made us to be in community with Him and in community with others. In addition, I am extremely competitive, and therefore I am always competing within myself, against myself, or against others, and that does not always make for productive friendships. And I, like you, am very busy and don't have a lot of time to make and develop friendships.

I have made a concerted effort to break from those obstacles and as I have dome so, I have found a huge stress reduction in my life as a result of those relationships. I have friends from my school years, and friends from my banking years with whom I have remained in contact. It is as if we can just pick up where we left off. I still communicate regularly with Jim Cossin, my best friend from seminary, and Dick Haynes, my best friend from my days at Westminster where we served together for twelve years.

There seem to be friends for certain seasons and places of life, which, even though you may not remain in close contact, when you see each other again it's like picking up where you left off.

Fifteen years ago, along came a very unlikely friend, Clint Kemp. Clint and I were thrown together at a conference as roommates. I say "unlikely" because Clint is my son's age and we are mirror opposites. We entered into an accountability relationship, and even though he lives in the Bahamas and I in Central Florida, we (I give most of the credit to his efforts) have maintained close continued contact over the years.

More recently here in Lake Mary, while I am fortunate to have some great acquaintances, I have several closer friends with whom I spend time regularly, meeting for lunch or golf, exchanging books, traveling with, or praying with. They include Tom Gwinn, Will Sydnor, Larry Harris, Larry Sherman, Brian Overby, and Tom Nelson. Those last two are my golf buddies who consistently *add* stress to my life each time they tee up from the tips and beat me like a drum.

And then there is my friend and golfing buddy Blair Culpepper. Blair and I met in the late sixties when I was a banker calling on his bank in Jacksonville. There was a long hiatus in our relationship, until Blair looked me up when he came to Minneapolis for a convention. He did this again when I was in Atlanta. Then when I moved to Orlando fifteen years ago to find him here, we picked up where we left off. Since then we have deepened the relationship many-fold. I would do anything for him.

Last year it was discovered that Blair had cancer. We both put on yellow "Livestrong" bracelets to remind us that we trusted the Lord to bring him through. He came through, and we took the bracelets off. The cancer came back, and back on came the bracelets. We met for lunch in August of that year to mark the end of his chemo/radiation treatments, and to celebrate we ceremoniously removed our bracelets. We have lunch together regularly and solve world problems and have been known to talk some sports. Blair is my best male Gator friend (actually I can't imagine having a better Seminole friend) and at present, he has the bragging rights. If he were with me right now, he'd remind me that he has had bragging rights for three years straight. That goes for my best female Gator friend, Cheryl Gwinn, as well.

Another feature added to my life since I've been in Lake Mary is being a part of a small group that meets weekly. My small group meets every Tuesday night from 7:00 to 9:00 p.m.

We eat, laugh, study the Bible, and then eat some more. I wouldn't miss it for anything, and judging from the regularity of attendance, nether would the others. In addition to our regular meetings, we pray for each other, help each other out when in need, and reach out to each other when we are sick or in some other way hurting. In short, we share life together. One of my mantras is that when people tell me they are too busy to be in a group, I tell them that's exactly why they need to be in a group. Again, beware of the barrenness of a busy life.

While these names may mean little or nothing to you, the friendships behind them hopefully remind you of those wonderful relationships that help reduce the stress in your life.

Let me share a couple of sermon illustrations that I have used over and over to illustrate the role of relationships in stress reduction.

We have all seen geese fly in the v-formation. The science of aerodynamics proves that they derive 77 percent more lift that way than if they flew horizontally or in a straight line. Furthermore, it is their instinctive habit for one to take the point (where the friction is the greatest) and then drop back to the end of one of the wings for rest while another takes its place. It's the same principle as drafting in NASCAR racing. We all need friends like these who will take the heat off us and for us, those who are willing to take the point while we draft (and vice versa).

Linda has been my best friend ever. I've known her since kindergarten, and we were best friends before we fell in love and became husband and wife. We are still best friends, and she frequently takes the point for me.

My children, too, have served as stress reducers. Seems like Fletcher (forty-four) and Ann (forty-one) have become more like good friends than children to Linda and me. We don't get to see Fletcher as often as we would like, as he lives in South Carolina. He is here for a week as I write. We've hung out together alone for five days. He, too, is a pastor, so we share lots of war stories together. For his fortieth birthday we went to Paris and London to celebrate and engage in some male bonding. This was a great get-away stress buster for us both.

Ann loves her daddy, as you would hope a daughter would. She is gifted with disarming humor and is a quiet and wise peacemaker who has put out many stress fires in my life. For her fortieth birthday last year we rented a house in Wellfleet at Cape Cod.

I once saw a study that talked about a scientist who put a monkey in a cage with a boa constrictor. He had the monkey all wired up to monitor his blood pressure, heart rate, and other vital signs. The poor little monkey's blood pressure was off the charts. But each time another monkey (also wired) was put in the cage, the reading subsided. And it struck me (figuratively speaking, of course) that the more monkeys we have in our stressful lives along with us, the less stressful our lives become!

Through these and other personal life applications, I am learning that in spite of my natural wiring to the contrary, my competitiveness and my busyness, I need people in my life.

I received a vivid reminder of this fact in reading *Into the Wild* by Jon Krakauer, the true story of a loner, Christopher Johnson McCandless, who ventures to Alaska, where he expects to escape from life and find "refuge in nature."[1] Yet McCandless wrote in his journal just before his death, "And so it turned out that only a life similar to the life around us, merging with it a ripple, is genuine life, and that an unshared happiness is not happiness."[2] Krakauer notes that McCandless then wrote, "Happiness only real when shared."[3]

Read these words in the Old Testament:

Two are better than one, because they have good return for their work; If one falls down, his friend can help him up. But pity the man who falls and has no one to help him up! Also, if two lie down together, they will keep warm. But how can one keep warm alone? Though

one may be overpowered, two can defend themselves.
A cord of three strands is not quickly broken.
—Ecclesiastes 4:9–12

Do you know how many tons one draft horse can pull?
Answer: two. Do you know how many tons two draft horses
can pull? You're not going to believe this. Answer: twenty-
three tons! Wow! That's awesome and should tell us loners
something about the power and strength in numbers that add
value to the old saying that two are better than one.

The Master who made us knows that we need to escape
every now and then in order for Him to regain His touch in
our lives.

Chapter 10

E Is for Escape

I am constantly running into people who feel trapped, and the best remedy I know is escape. There are many healthy ways to escape from it all and return to whatever you escaped from with a fresh, new perspective.

Just as there are different strokes for different folks, there are different escapes for different folks.

For me, the longest and strongest escape mechanism has been jogging. I started jogging thirty-five years ago. Today I jog two times a week, early in the morning for the solitude, coolness, and safety. (There are few cars at five in the a.m.)

At this point I feel the need as a protective husband and father to add a note to my women readers. I caution jogging or engaging in other forms of outdoor public exercise alone. Unfortunately, we don't live in a society where women and children are always assured of safety when they are alone.

Some people jog for health reasons, but for me this is merely a side benefit, as I do it for working off stress. I don't understand physiology, but there is something about endorphins being released into the body with a good cardiovascular workout that makes my day. It gets the blood flowing, I eat better, sleep better, and think more clearly.

Jogging isn't for everybody. It seems like certain body types take best to jogging, like small, light folks. But you'd be surprised how many joggers, like me, don't necessarily fit that description. One half-hour at a conversational pace and you are at about where you want to be in terms of exercise efficiency. After that, the law of diminishing returns sets in. I used to jog everyday, and then I started listening to my body telling me that too much of a good thing makes Johnny a tired and sometimes an achy little boy. As such, the enjoyment started to decrease and it seemed more like work than fun. So, I cut back to every other day, which gave my aging body time to recover and beg for more.

Three years ago I was getting a little bored with the every-other-day routine (by the way, another good tip for those of you who may decide to give running a try, vary the course and it will make it more enjoyable), so I decided to buy a bike, which I have been riding once a week. This has been just the change I was looking for in the routine. It is cooler biking than jogging (more air rushes over your body), and you can go as far or fast as you like—race like a mad man or merely meander and explore. I've learned more about the thirty-mile radius around my house in the last five years than I learned in the previous twelve combined. If you choose this route, it helps if your area has bike trails or at least bike lanes on some of the roads you travel. There is no substitute for a good seat, good riding pants with six or eight-ply to cushion your tush, and gloves to keep you from getting numb-hand. Whatever equipment you get, a helmet is the most critical. You can easily outfit yourself with a decent bike and all the above for less than one thousand dollars. If you aren't planning to ride very far, say, just around the neighborhood, then it will be one-fourth that amount. Make sure you keep the right amount of pressure in your tires at all times, and you are in for one of the great stress reducers of all time!

Golf also has been a long-standing hobby of mine. While I enjoy golf when I'm playing well, it can be a major source of stress if I'm not. (Maybe you are one of the people I admire who can go out and have a great time on the golf course no matter what you shoot. Good for you; I haven't arrived there yet). To play well you need to play often. To play often you need to devote at least a half of a day and twenty to forty-five dollars, neither of which I find it easy to do. Therefore, golf has taken a back seat in my escape plan.

Another escape is the banjo. Unfortunately because I am cursed with a love for music but an inability to reproduce it, it has been laid aside out of frustration and the stress it causes when it was meant for relaxation.

Reading was not my first love, but has always been that of my wife (she will read several books a week), but I have grown to love reading as a means of escape. Novels are my thing. Give me Ken Follett, Stuart Woods, John Grisham, Patricia Cornwell, George MacDonald, Tom Perry, Carl Hiaasen, and lately since I've read everything these have written, I'm looking for more good novelists. If it's not novels, then Charles Swindoll, Max Lucado, Gordon MacDonald, Philip Yancy, John Piper, R. C. Sproul, and of course my main man, Steve Brown. If you haven't read any of Steve's books, you are in for a tell-it-like-it-is treat. In addition to being refreshingly honest, Steve's writings will lead you to the freedom for which you have been looking.

It's been said before and I'll say it again, books are our friends. These friends, too, afford me inexpressible escape from the stress of life.

Thus far, my concentration on escapes has been on the doing of something: jogging, bicycling, golfing, and reading; but I'll be the first to say that there is no substitute for just being at the ocean or in the mountains. I can sit, listen to the constant pounding of the waves, and stare endlessly at the vastness of the ocean, and before long I'm healed of stress. I can sit by a fire and stare endlessly at the majesty of the Great Smoky Mountains, and before long I am transported to another place far away from the stresses of life.

Find a safe place to escape and watch the stress fall away. For lack of better word, *retreat*.

One of the places where I have gone on occasion is to the Monastery of the Holy Spirit in Conyers, Georgia. It sits on huge acreage and provides Spartan accommodations for a mere donation. (The last time I was there it was a suggested forty dollars per day.) Meals are taken in silence. It's silence everywhere, and it's maddening at first; then once you settle into it you begin to get in touch with yourself again and then you begin to see what the monks see in this quiet life in the slow lane. Then you begin to ache for what you've left as you realize that this life is for the monks and not for you, except occasionally.

The *Orlando Sentinel* had a great article by Kate Santich entitled "Pause and push 'refresh'" that said, "In a productivity-obsessed culture, some still take time to do, well, nothing."[1] The article went on to quote a local psychologist, Dr. Alan Keck, who relative to the struggle of getting people to take twenty minutes a day for relaxation and meditation says, "We know that it slows down brain waves, provides a kind of relaxation that is different in some ways than sleep, and is restorative not only mentally but physically too. It reduces anxiety, improves mood, improves the immune system and the body's ability to heal itself, lowers blood pressure—I could go on and on."[2] Each day for the past three and one-half decades, Dr. Keck has lain in a hammock and spends twenty minutes meditating.

In her article, Ms. Santich makes note of the fact that in our culture, such is looked down on as lazy, overindulging, slacker behaviors not to be emulated. Don't give in to such criticism, which in my experience comes from misery-loves-company folks suffering from stress overloads. Another source quoted in her article is Janet Luhrs, author of *The Simple Living Guide*, who among other things suggests starting one's day with silence by reading something inspirational.[3]

It has been my practice to read from the Bible for almost forty years, and I honestly believe I can tell the difference the days I neglect this practice.

One last thing I will mention is that I love cutting my yard. Let me tell you why. In my calling I don't sweat much, unless it is of the nervous variety. I am indoors a lot in my work. And, the other biggest reason I like to cut my yard is that in my line of work, I can't often see measurable results. I mean I will put in twelve to eighteen hours preparing a sermon, but it is hard to tell what effect it has. But when I cut my yard, I can see instant results: it looked bad when I started and good when I finished. We all need something that provides the clear result and gratification of a job well done. Build things like that into your life, and your stress levels will go down.

Hear me. Don't wait until you grow older like I am to stop and smell the coffee. Don't make all the hollow excuses I did as to why I couldn't break away. I've got nobody to blame but myself for not doing this sooner and more often. Hear me.

What is your escape route? If you don't have one, find one before you completely stress out. Gardening, bird watching, woodworking, working on cars, making crafts, Sudoku, whatever—find something and or some place that takes you away from it all.

Chapter 11

S Is for Spending

Ihesitate to address this topic for fear that what I'm about to write will come across simplistically old hat. But I am reminded that when the boys of summer go into spring training, they work on pitching, running, and catching—the fundamentals. And there are certain timeless fundamentals that need be kept in mind in the area of spending if we are to reduce stress in this area of our lives. The Master's hand guiding us into sound stewardship principles is needed in the spending area if we are to reduce the stress in our lives caused by improper spending.

American's spending patterns changed for the worse with the inception of installment loans and credit cards. While there are those who would disagree, I trace the origin of today's consumerism to these two spending features.

Installment loans were originated to help the soldiers when they returned from World War II. Credit cards were a natural extension of the installment loan concept of buying now and paying later. I was in the banking business in the sixties when credit cards started to make their move. I was on both the lending side as a banker and the spending side as a consumer.

On the lending side, we as lenders began to see the consumer's abuse, which was fostered by the credit card companies and credit card holders alike. The credit card companies knew a good thing, profit-wise, when they saw it. And boy could they see it with the 18 percent interest rates (not to mention the annual fee they charge cardholders) they charged on the unpaid balances of the undisciplined credit card holders who did not pay off their balances every thirty days. In addition, something that few of us give thought is that the credit card companies engage in double dipping as they charge a fee to the businesses from whom we purchase. (And don't you think that these businesses tack this fee on to their merchandise and thereby pass this fee on to the cardholders? You know they do!) As a lender, I witnessed folks getting overextended, having been issued multiple credit cards, which the cardholders began using to rob Peter and pay Paul.

Credit card companies would say that I'm being unfairly critical. They would likely use the illustration that the credit card is a useful instrument of service and convenience and is analogous to the remote TV control, i.e., it's in the user's hands to be used responsibly. The credit card companies would say they are not to blame for making this service available but it's the irresponsibility of the users that is the problem.

Using the credit card as a debit card is also feeding the banking institutions huge profits and taking money out of the user's pockets. *Newsweek's* Jane Bryant Quinn wrote an article in 2006 in which she stated that overall debit cards are less expensive to use than credit cards, for which you carry over a balance.[1] Just be aware of the excessive bank fees for getting cash advances.

Yes, indeed, the user is finally to blame, but to give some users a credit card is like putting a drink in the hands of an alcoholic. Debt plays into the hands of our base nature, which is looking for instant gratification. Few of us exercise the financial discipline to not spend more than we make. Few of us exercise the discipline to not buy what we don't need. Someone once said that he who buys what he does not need, steals from himself.

Banks, credit card companies, and other lending institutions charge off tons of money every year and still make tons more. I can remember a time while in the banking business when we realized we weren't losing enough money. You heard me correctly. Our charge off or credit card loss rate was lower than the national average, so we made a concerted effort to approve more cards, knowing that when we did so we would lose more money but we would make far more than we would lose. Have you ever heard of any credit card company going out of business? No, but you sure have heard of the rising number of personal bankruptcies, haven't you?

I remember quickly piling up four thousand dollars in credit card debt and making only the minimum monthly payments. (And that was in 1960s dollars, which would be approximately ten times that in today's dollars.) I can still recall experiencing the stress of that mounting debt. Since it has been our practice for me to handle the finances, it was right there before me staring me in the face each month. My guess is that in your family the one who juggles the books has the most financially related stress, and your spouse is somewhat in the dark as to just how deep the financial weeds are. My guess is that the one who cooks the books in your family is keeping the bad news from the other to spare them the worry. My guess is that the one who is not doing the finances in the family has an idea that the family is skating on thin ice, but really doesn't want to know just how bad it is. I hope I'm a bad guesser. Only you know.

So there we were, living the American Dream. I had a wife, two children, a house payment (now you can even borrow on your home equity, which ought to be saved up for retirement instead), a car payment (most of us are what the lenders call upside-down, meaning we owe more on the car than it is worth), and credit card debt that was inconceivable to pay off. If you added up all the payments, utility bills, doctor bills, gasoline bills, grocery bills, insurance bills, and other routine monthly expenses, we were overextended and paid out more than we took in. Sound familiar? We were like the proverbial person sinking in a sea of debt up to our bottom lip, and God forbid if an emergency arose. Never mind how we would pay for Christmas or a vacation.

Talk about stress! Yikes! Stop the world; I want to get off!

Fortunately we were able to right the financial ship when I left the bank, as we cashed out our profit-sharing plan and applied it to forever pay off the credit card debt. As smart as this is in reducing or paying off expensive debt, it also reduces the retirement nest egg as well. For more than thirty years now we have had the habit of paying off our credit card balance every thirty days. That's how you spell relief. I can't tell you how much less stress there is as a result of that one decision.

Like most of you, I have had a struggle deciphering between needs and wants. I have come over the years to slowly learn that there is quite a difference. Therein is another problem.

One of the smartest things I've heard regarding needs and wants is to wait thirty days before making any major purchases. I will leave it up to you to decide what is major and what is not.

One area where I need to improve is in the area of buying new cars. For one thing, in order to not get upside-down on your car loan, put a minimum of 25 percent or more down. I like new, but new isn't the smartest way to go. The minute you drive your shiny new car off the showroom floor it depreciates. It is better to buy a good pre-owned car from a reputable dealer. I have a friend who put me in touch with a mechanic who will inspect a used car with a fine-toothed comb for fifty dollars. It might be the best fifty bucks you can spend.

Another little helpful device is to accrue expenses. For instance, I pay my car insurance every six months. Therefore, what I do is subtract one-sixth of the insurance bill every month out of my bank balance and when it comes time to pay my insurance bill in July and January of each year, it is already there. You can do this with Christmas, vacation, birthday presents, estimated taxes, and the like. Another helpful hint is to accrue insurance deductibles. If, for instance, your health insurance deductible is five hundred dollars and you have a major medical expense early in the year, it is all out-of-pocket expenses. If you accrue, then it's there and won't hit you so hard. Try it and you'll be surprised how easy it will become and how much of a stress reliever it is.

We've already seen the wisdom of preparing a time budget; now let's talk about budgeting in its normal context. Budgets tell your money where to go instead of wondering where it went. I suggest that at least you and your spouse sit down together and prepare a budget. You may want to expand this to include your children, depending on their ages. I also recommend (at whatever age you deem appropriate) that you establish a budget for your children in order to teach them the value of money and financial responsibility.

Budgeting is not rocket science. There is how much is coming in (income) and how much is going out (expenses), and if there is a positive difference, it is called discretionary income. Get your check register before you so as to more easily recall the nature and amount of expenditures you have made over a considerable period of time. The only way to adjust your budget is to make more or spend less, or a combination of the two. That is true for the Montgomerys, the United States government (no great example of financial responsibility with a debt in the trillions), the Gateses, a church, or General Motors. The principle works the same for all.

Once you have established your budget, then tweak it as necessary to more accurately reflect your circumstances. Then stick to it. Once you get into the flow of budgeting, you will soon see that there is money left over at the end of the month instead of too much month left over at the end of your money.

I cannot recommend highly enough the twelve-week course offered by Crown Financial Ministries. The course is offered all over the country and world in several languages. Contact Crown and ask for the teaching location nearest you.

What is your long-range plan for retirement? Do you even have one? You better because if you don't, you will not likely be living out your later years on the same financial level you are living now. Waiting on an inheritance? My friend Will Sydnor, who is an estate tax lawyer, tells me that those who are fortunate enough to have an inheritance come their way spend 90 percent of it in the first six months. Inheritors beware! Will's statement is backed up in a September 2006 *Orlando Sentinel* article entitled, "Don't hit the skids after hitting the big jackpot." In this article, Gregory Karp of *The (Allentown) Morning Call* quotes from the National

Endowment for Financial Education, which says 70 percent of people who receive large lump sums of money blow it in a few years.[2] The article cited a woman who received a multimillion-dollar settlement stemming from her husband's death as a result of 9/11. Shortly thereafter, she had approximately half a million left.

Chapter 12

S Is for Shepherd

Did you hear the story about the person who called his pastor with a stress problem? His pastor replied, "Take two psalms and call me in the morning." Now, I'm not sure which two psalms I would recommend if I had only two to prescribe, but I do know what one of them would be. It would be my first choice, as it has been of so many others for so many years—Psalm 23, which in the New International Version is translated as follows:

> The Lord is my shepherd, I shall not be in want. He makes me lie down in green pastures, he leads me beside quiet waters, he restores my soul. He guides me in paths of righteousness for his name's sake. Even though I walk through the valley of the shadow of death, I will fear no evil, for you are with me; your rod and your staff, they comfort me. You prepare a table before me in the presence of my enemies. You anoint my head with oil; my cup overflows. Surely goodness and love will follow me all the days of my life, and I will dwell in the house of the Lord forever.

It is now time to learn the song of those who stress less.

For the uninitiated, Psalm 23 was written by the greatest songwriter of his day or some would say of any day, a man named David. His songs don't have titles, just numbers. Some say he played a pretty mean harp. He always had one or more of his songs in the top forty of his day. None of these hit singles were ever copyrighted, nor did David ever make a penny off of them. David was a wealthy man and didn't need the royalties. While David was a wealthy man, he was richer in his relationship with his Shepherd, whom he obviously enjoyed very much. All his songs are in the public domain for us all to enjoy.

David himself was a shepherd in his early years, which qualifies him to write about the relationship between a shepherd and his sheep. Note that this is a very personal song. There are 115 words, 24 percent of which are personal pronouns. This personal tone resonates with the chapter on relationships. It is an inescapable fact that this Shepherd loves His sheep very much.

Isn't that the ultimate measure of caring? In our culture we take photography for granted. We see pictures of others all the time, especially of our loved ones. My sister, Severy, just sent me some things of my dad's that she had come across and thought I would like. One of them was a picture of my dad. Wouldn't it be nice to have a picture of God? But how do you take a picture of the One who is Spirit form? Well, David does a pretty good job of giving us one in song twenty-three. We say a picture is worth a thousand words, but I say, these 115 words are worth more than a picture of God.

The book from which I have benefited the most in my understanding of Song 23 is Philip Keller's *A Shepherd Looks at Psalm 23*. I learned a new appreciation for Psalm 23 as a result of reading his wonderfully insightful book. Keller, who was for a time a shepherd, brought to this city boy a fresh appreciation of what the shepherd, David, sang before him. Many of the insights I have gained from Keller I will now share with you as we look together at Song 23.

The Lord Is My Shepherd[1]

Who is your shepherd? Or to put the question in more modern terminology, who do you completely trust to manage your life? Who do you acknowledge as being in control? My guess is that most who read this would think it an odd question. However odd, I think it not merely an important one, but perhaps the most important question that we can ask.

One option, probably the most popular option, is that most of us trust ourselves first and foremost. This is called humanism. Some see humanism as a religion unto itself. In humanistic thinking, man sees himself as being the captain of his own ship and the master of his own fate. My observation of this humanism is that it has failed as a religion. It always has and always will because however good God made us, we always will fail God and ourselves. Are you totally pleased with the way you have managed your life? If you are honest, you will answer as I will: no. We are not such great captains, are we? We have not even measured up to our own standards, have we?

How about you, what is your say in the matter?

I've known quite a few religious people who with all sincerely have believed that God helps those who help themselves. Quite a few of these believed they were quoting the Bible. There is no such verse. Quite to the contrary, the teaching of the Scriptures on the subject is best summarized by the idea that we, like sheep, are all helpless and that God is our willing and able Helper or Shepherd.

Another option that we must humbly accept is that we find it necessary from time to time and for one reason or another to trust others. In the act of doing so we freely admit that we are not totally in control inasmuch as we must depend on others.

There are a number of people to whom we entrust our care and that of our possessions as well.

When I fly on an airplane I entrust my safety, care, and yes, my life, to the hands of mechanics, air traffic controllers, and the all-important pilots, none of whom I personally know. I entrust the care of my city, county, state, and nation to many who serve me in their various capacities from collecting my garbage to running the country and defending it. Most of these I don't know either. Doctors, nurses, and hospitals play a major role in our care. Retirement and nursing homes, too. Financial planners, brokers, insurance agents, lawyers, and counselors are among those in whom we place our trust. Priests, rabbis, and pastors, too.

Rather than asking who your shepherd is, perhaps caregiver, trustee, or guardian would relate better. We commonly turn to others to care for us. The earliest example is that of a child who is entrusting their well-being to their parents (or guardian). There is also the example of an elderly person who entrusts their care to another for their well-being, such as my dear ninety-year-old mother, Cathrine, who is increasingly entrusting her care to me. These examples tend to illustrate the beginnings and endings of care in life.

We trust in places and institutions (homes, governments, merchants, or sports teams). They do not meet our expectations, and we become stressed. We trust in things (clothes, cars, furniture, or jewelry), and they break, rust, wear out, get flat tires, the batteries run down, they get stolen or lost, and we are stressed out. We trust in events (parties, conferences, books, vacations, and holidays), and they don't meet our expectations and we become stressed.

I could go on and on, but it is not uncommon for us to place our trust in others in the routine of life. As unavoidable and necessary as it is, when we do so, we invite even more stress into our lives because those to whom we entrust our care sometimes betray our trust.

We trust in people (spouses, children, parents, friends, in-laws, employers, employees, and others mentioned above). When they let us down, we are stressed.

My wife and I recently experienced one such occasion. Our front door needed replacing, along with the side panels. A young man who was doing some other work for us gave us every assurance that he could reframe the door, replace all the rotten wood with pressure-treated wood and seal it up tight as a drum. Foolishly, I trusted his word. Not only am I out approximately six hundred dollars, but the door was not done well and we are now contracting with someone else to do it right this time.

Another plausible option is to merely think that everything is a matter of chance, luck or happenstance (hap for luck), chaos, or simply a matter of fate. In other words, it doesn't really matter what we do, whether we trust ourselves, or what others do that we trust. If any of these are true, then it's a jungle out there and it's every man for himself. Unfortunately some seem to live their lives as though this is what they believe. This adds even more stress to our world.

None of these options engender security in anyone or anything. No wonder there is so much insecurity in this world and its peoples. This insecurity breeds stress.

All this amounts to the proverbial catch-22. If we trust in ourselves; others; or merely write it all off to fate, luck, or chaos, the result is the same—stress.

Sounds pretty dismal, doesn't it?

What is the answer?

Is there an answer?

Let me propose an option other than those posed above, one better than totally trusting yourself, totally trusting others, or not trusting anyone or anything because life has no rhyme or reason. The option I have chosen is to completely let go and trust in the Lord, turning over the management and leadership of my life to Him.

We start out as children trusting in others to care for us. We are totally dependent upon others, and this is understandable. However, at some point we need to make the shift from trusting in God's creatures to trusting in God Himself. This is not a shift most of us make, and as a result we invite unnecessary stress into our lives. Note that the words in David's song ("The Lord is my shepherd") come as it were from the mouth of one of the shepherd's sheep.

Before I share with you how to place your trust in the Lord, if you have not already done so, let's examine why He should be worthy of such trust and specifically what it is we can trust Him for. If you have already placed your trust in the Lord, then this ought to serve as a wonderful reminder why.

Let me say at this point that the greatest decision I ever made was when He led me to turn over the management or control of my life to Him, and I did! He is my number one priority in life and I identify with the sheep in Song 23. This has been the single most important decision of my life in terms of reducing stress or learning to cope with stress.

Come, let us bow down in worship, let us kneel before the Lord our Maker; for he is our God and we are the people of his pasture, the flock under his care.
—Psalm 95:6–7

Know that the Lord is God. It is he who made us, and we are his; we are his people, the sheep of his pasture.
—Psalm 100:3

Green Pastures, Quiet Waters, Anointing, and Overflowing Cups

Let's take an active look at the sheep's perspective from David's eyes. David had the unique perspective of being a shepherd to sheep. And after having worked with sheep, David could see the humiliating and sometimes unflattering similarities between these sheep and himself and us all. For instance, sheep are not naturally content creatures. Sound familiar? See the similarity?

David learned the simple truth that a sheep's well-being and even its life was completely, totally and absolutely dependent on the care of a good shepherd. David learned from experience that sheep cannot take good care of themselves, nor will they take good care of each other. David leaned the hard truth from other shepherds and other flocks that bad shepherds who didn't properly care for their sheep left their sheep to ruin, even die.

Due to the similarity of the care rendered by the Shepherd in the verse about green pastures and quiet waters and the verses that deal with anointing and the overflowing cup, these verses will be treated together. All we like sheep need green pastures or a place to lie down in peace and large quantities of quiet (remember the chapter on escape?) or still waters from which we may rehydrate our bodies, lest we become dehydrated. Furthermore, when frightened or annoyed, we shy away from lying down to rest and from troubled waters, even at the expense of growing tired and going thirsty.

The anatomy of sheep is very similar to that of a human. The body weight of both humans and sheep consist of 70 percent fluid. Sheep desperately need water. Three days without fluids and a human can die. Is it any wonder then that one of the first things David mentions regarding the well-being of a sheep is water?

Sheep are spooky, too. I think my dog, Caleb, must be part sheep. My wife, Linda, too. To be perfectly honest, I'm not as impervious to fear as I let on. I don't like things that go bump in the night any more than you do. Yes, I'm the one who gets up and scouts out the source of the bump, but believe me, it's not because I am brave. Sheep aren't brave, either. Without the shepherd's constant vigil, the sheep feel more insecure from fearsome predators that lurk in the shadows waiting for the right time to pounce. Intuitively the sheep know they are out there somewhere, but they also must know the comfort of their nearby shepherd or they will be too stressed to lie down or drink.

All these factors and other discomforting factors contribute to sheep losing their appetite and weight loss. They need rest from these factors before they will eat, and they can't eat even when rested if the shepherd doesn't provide green pastures for them. Green pastures just don't happen. Shepherds need to lead their sheep to the green pastures. This means moving the sheep in the spring from the lowlands where they have been wintering to the highlands where the greener pastures are waiting for them. The shepherd must go ahead of them to painstakingly remove poisonous plants and other potentially harmful things of which the sheep are unaware of but prove a threat to their well-being.

By now we are growing in our appreciation of the tender, loving care of a shepherd who takes his job seriously. We are not through yet. To add to what has already been said, we must mention that water is not necessarily to be found in abundance. Somehow in my ignorance concerning sheep, I just thought that there were rivers, streams, ponds, and pools everywhere in abundance from which they could elect to drink. Furthermore, if water is available, it does not necessarily mean the sheep will drink even if they are dying of thirst. Why? If the river is a rushing torrent, not quiet or still, then they will not go near it out of fear.

If the embankment is too steep, then they are in peril of falling in. On top of that there are times when they are so thirsty that they will drink out of puddles of mud and the urine and feces of other sheep. Therefore the shepherd must sometimes get the water for them himself by drawing a cup out of the torrent or by going down into a well. The thirsty sheep drink to their delight from the overflowing cup provided by the shepherd. Once again, little does the sheep know or even appreciate the extent to which his shepherd has gone to provide this life-saving water. Like sheep, we have a cup that needs filling, a cup that without the help of another greater than ourselves will remain less than full.

Sheep are like us in another way. It is not so much the big, growling predators that cause them stress as much as the annoying, little, pesky things, like flies, which can literally bug them to death. A particularly persistent mosquito can stress me out rather well. I'll never forget my first summer in Minneapolis, wherein I encountered my first mosquitoes in the north. There are two standard jokes about Minnesota. The first is that there are two seasons in Minneapolis: winter and July; the other is that there are two seasons in Minneapolis: good ice fishing and bad ice fishing. Mosquitoes there are huge and fly in formation with a pint of blood under each wing. OK, a slight hyperbole, but then I saw a T-shirt with a mosquito on it with the words "Minnesota State Bird" and I knew I wasn't exaggerating.

Is there anything more annoying when you are trying to get to sleep than the incessant noise of a mosquito flying overhead? The answer to that question is, Yes, there is something more annoying: when the noise stops; for when it stops, you can be sure you are unwillingly donating blood and that it is not going to the Red Cross.

One of the eternal questions is, Why did God make mosquitoes? While I am on this side bar, there are other haunting questions like, Where do the handkerchiefs go? and, Where does the other sock go? Oh, the unsolvable mysteries of life!

The July 14, 2006, *Orlando Sentinel* reported on sixteen-year-old phenom Michele Wie, who hit the golfing world with a bang.[2] She has yet to win on the women's tour, but has had three close seconds and looks poised to break through any time. Another of her goals is to at least make the cut in a tournament on the men's tour. When she does it will be the first time in sixty-one years. At the time of the article's publication, her next big opportunity was to be the John Deere Classic. After shooting an opening round 77, it appears she will have to wait. It turns out that her problems were more mental than physical. She forgot her insect repellant, a rookie mistake. The article said, "(Wie) was bugged by those little pests that populate Midwest golf courses...'I mean, I literally had like five of them on me,' said Wie...'As soon as I as I got on the ball—I mean, it's OK if the bugs are like around the ball. I can handle that. But they were crawling on my arm, they were on my hand, they were on my head. It was just ridiculous. I had to step back like five times. It was just very unfortunate. I would like to say it didn't, but it bothered me a little bit. Bugs on me, I hate bugs, and I was starting to get a little bit aggravated like the fifth time I stepped out [meaning stepping away from hitting the ball]. Wie then proceeded to hit her tee shot in the water hazard, which led to one of her many costly bogeys for the day."[3]

Shepherds care for their sheep by anointing their heads with oil. I have already alluded to the flies and other pesky critters that are more than bothersome to the sheep. The favorite spot for the botfly is the sheep's nose cavity, where they lay their eggs. These eggs can hatch and go right to the brain and drive them crazy, literally. To prevent this, the shepherd will take a solution and apply it to their nose, which action repels the flies.

I can relate to the sheep being bugged inasmuch as when I near the finish of a morning jog, the deer flies bombard me. I must look like a nut waving my hands about my head and neck (seemingly their favorite targets), and let me tell you they can leave a bite that will emit a poison that stays in the bite area for a week.

Sheep become easily stressed within their ranks as well. They too, like other species, have a butting order. During mating season, the Monarch rams' necks swell and they head butt. In order to combat this problem, the shepherd will anoint these rams with grease all over their heads so that when they butt heads, they glance off of one another. This causes them to become frustrated, and then they quit butting.

I watched the finals of the 2002 World Cup, wherein Italy defeated France in a hard-fought contest. This Cup forever will be remembered for Zinedine Zidane, aka ZiZou, the top French player of his generation, receiving a red card ejection from the match for head butting Italy's Marco Materazzi with ten minutes remaining in the thirty-minute extra time period. The match was level at 1, the French goal having been scored by ZiZou on a penalty kick. France went on to lose in a penalty shootout. The lesson? Head butting is not restricted to sheep—I know, I've taken and given a few myself.

I neglected to tell you about one of my golf buddies. He, like the others I mentioned, is a good golfer. And we, too, play for honor of Top Gun. Whoever said playing with good golfers makes you a better golfer never played with this guy. We have a friendly head-butting thing going, inasmuch as the loser of each round gets this purple tee with the woman's name, *Myrtle R. Mulligan* on it. I don't know where we found it or who *Myrtle R. Mulligan* is, but I do know that nine times out of ten I have the tee in my possession at the end of the round. As a matter of fact, I have it in my possession as I write—more stress that requires anointing.

Marriages have ended because of head butts. People have lost their jobs, including a few pastors I know, for butting heads with those in their company or congregation. For these and other reasons, the Lord has given the anointing of His Spirit so that we can keep our heads about us when others are losing theirs.

I vividly recall as a youngster growing up in church were we sang the song "There Is a Balm in Gilead." At that time our country was concluding World War II with the terribly frightening hydrogen bomb. In my uneducated mind I was unable at that time to discern between the words *balm* and *bomb*. Therefore I was confused to say the least, regarding how Jesus—the "Bomb" of Gilead—was going to cure sin-sick souls and make the wounded whole, when the only balm I was familiar with was spelled and pronounced *bomb*! Fortunately, I'm older and wiser now, and I have come to know the difference between a balm and a bomb. By God's grace, I now understand that Jesus is the *Balm*!

Right Paths and Soul Restoration

The trip from the lowlands to the highlands and back again before winter is not without its challenges as well. The sheep don't know the way, but the shepherd does. The sheep get lost, but never the Shepherd, for He is the Way. That's why He confidently says, "Follow Me" (Matt. 4:19).

If not watched carefully, sheep will wander off, whether it's on the journey or at rest. Sound familiar? Many bad things can happen to them when they wander off. Sound familiar? For one thing they are easier prey alone than when amongst the flock, just like the women that I advise not to jog alone. Remember the chapter on relationships and the quote from Ecclesiastes? For another, they can get in places they can't get out of. Sound familiar? Because of their wool (some liken their wool to our pride...observe the middle letter in the word pride), they can become entangled in the brush. When I am drifting off where I don't belong, doing my own thing, I more easily become entangled in the thickets of life. Also, because of the nature of the sheep's body (picture a sheep for a second with its big torso and disproportionately small legs) it can easily lose its balance, fall down, and not be able to right itself (somewhat like an SUV rollover). Sometimes sheep will lie in a depression (and I don't use that term loosely) on the ground, roll on their side, and not be able to get up. This common condition is called being cast down. A watchful shepherd will notice when one of his sheep is cast down and will quickly come to its aid, for if he does not either the sheep will be attacked in its helpless condition or merely die of the gas build up in its body.

Humans, too, become cast down or downcast (see Songs 42 and 43 for David's use of this term). Like with sheep, this most often happens when we lose our way (in pursuit of greener grass, perhaps) or just simply get too comfortable for our own good.

Whenever I think of greener pastures, I am reminded of a painting that hung in the home of one of the church members in Minneapolis. It depicted four cows, each in their separate, fenced-in pen of lush grass, each eating through the fence of another cow.

Why does the grass always seem greener in some one else's pasture?

As with sheep and the shepherd, so too with us and the Lord. He constantly watches over His own, knows who is AWOL or downcast, and comes a-running like the police on an Amber Alert or paramedics on a 911 call after His lost or endangered sheep.

All we, like sheep, go off on the wrong paths and get out of sorts by all sorts of other things, which I will mention momentarily. As such, out of sorts, we are stressed out. We need to be redirected to a better path. We need to be restored.

What's got you down? Do you feel like the sheep just described above? Helpless? Afraid? Unable to right yourself?

When I find myself downcast, I immediately call my 911—the Lord, my Shepherd—He comes once again. You'd think He'd give up on me by now, but no, He can't, simply because I am His own and He is 100 percent committed to my care. Why is He so committed? Because His good name,

His reputation, is on the line! Therefore, if for no other reason than because of His name's sake, He will see to my well-being. In another part of God's Word (John 10), the Lord, who is my Shepherd, says that a hired hand will abandon his sheep, but not Him. A part of that commitment is to pick me up when I fall, steady my legs, put me on the right path once again and thereby restore my soul.

As the shepherd leads his sheep from the lowlands to the highlands, he will necessarily lead them through valleys often so low that the mountains above block out the sun. Therefore the deep valleys through which the sheep must pass will be dark as night. In daylight the footing would be treacherous, but in the shadows it is even more dangerous. There is simply no way around these valleys any more than there is a way around some of the valleys through which we must pass in our own lives. Some stress is unavoidable. All we, like sheep, go through the dark valleys of life, which exacerbates our normal tendency of fear. We need someone to walk with us through thick and thin.

Shadowy Valley

We all, like sheep, find ourselves in dark places in life.

Remember in the darkness what He taught you in the light.

The main thing he has taught us in the light is: Fear not. (God speaks the phrase "Fear not" more than any other phrase in the Scriptures—366 times, in fact!) Why? Simple. Because we, like sheep, are scaredy cats.

In my experience as a pastor, Song 23 is hands-down the most frequently requested scripture at the time of a funeral. (And it is almost always printed in the handout prepared by the funeral home.) It may surprise you that this part of the song has nothing to do with death. This is not to say that we will not die one day, and when we do it may be in a valley; and then again it may not. These valleys and the dark, ominous shadows they cast may have the feel and a fear similar to death, but notice that the song states I walk through, meaning that I don't die there but survive the experience.

The good news of this passage is in the words and the reality, "For You are with me." He's the one responsible for taking you into the valley (the exception to this is that this may be a valley of your own choosing or making; a path that was not righteous. And even though he did not lead you into it, if you look to him, he will lead you out) and he will be responsible to get you through. For all of you reading this that are in the shadow of a frightening valley of life, take heart. With the Good Shepherd's help, you will emerge from the shadows. This may be a trial or test from the Lord, which will make you stronger and wiser. As you do become stronger and wiser you will see the light of day once again and will be led to your next destination.

His Voice

More than likely the sheep are traveling single file, unable in the dark to see their shepherd, so how do they know the shepherd is with them? The answer is that he leads them by his voice and sometimes whistles or makes other noises with his mouth with which the sheep are familiar and therefore comforted.

Babies in the womb become acquainted with the voices of their parents even before they come out of this dark place. The baby is most familiar with its mother's voice simply because it is the one it hears more than any other.

In another part of Scripture, John 10:27 and 29, we read about the Good Shepherd. It is in this passage wherein we hear the voice of our Lord, who says, "My sheep listen to my voice; I know them, and they follow me...no one can snatch them out of my Father's hand."

In a similar way, God maintains contact with His people through His voice as recorded in the Bible. Whether I am walking in a shadow or in the lowlands or on a mountaintop, one of the ways I am confident of His presence is by listening to His voice in His Word. It is my intention that this be a daily practice, not a religious duty, but a joyful encounter with the voice of the living God.

One of my favorite Bible passages when I need to listen to His voice is:

> Therefore I tell you, do not worry about your life, what you will eat or drink; or about your body, what you will wear. Is not life more important than food, and the body more important than clothes? Look at the birds of the air; they do not sow or reap or store away in barns, and yet your heavenly Father feeds them. Are you not much more valuable than they? Who of you by worrying can add a single hour to his life? And why do you worry about clothes? See how the lilies of the field grow. They do not labor or spin. Yet I tell you that not even Solomon in all his splendor was dressed like one of these. If that is how God clothes the grass of the field, which is here today and tomorrow is thrown into the fire, will he not much more clothe you, O you of little faith? So do not worry, saying, "What shall we eat?" or "What shall we drink?" or "What shall we wear?" For the pagans run after all these things, and your heavenly Father knows that you need them. But seek first his kingdom and his righteousness, and all these things will be given to you as well. Therefore do not worry about tomorrow, for tomorrow will worry about itself. Each day has enough trouble of its own.
> —Matthew 6:25–34

Would you like to hear the voice of the One who created you and sustains your life, the voice of God Himself? Then pick up the Bible and read. If this has never been your practice, then I suggest that you read some of the songs in the Book of Psalms. If you want to read about the Good Shepherd, then find the Book of John. I will personally be surprised if after reading those twenty-one chapters you will not hunger and thirst for more. Maybe it used to be your practice to read

God's Word but you have fallen out of practice. You already know the benefits of hearing God's voice, and all you need is this reminder, which will be worth far more than the price of my book.

His Rod and His Staff

Another common means by which the shepherd maintains contact with his flock is by his rod (picture a baton or club) and his staff (picture the shepherd's crook).

The shepherd uses his rod and his staff to for a variety of purposes. His rod is often used as a defensive weapon that was thrown with great accuracy at the predators of his flock. Sometimes the shepherd uses it to separate the wool of his sheep in order to inspect their skin for scabs, which can spread and infect the entire flock. Other times the shepherd throws his rod just on the other side of a sheep who is straying in an effort to draw it back into contact with the others, similar to when you throw a rock into a pond just beyond a toy boat that has floated out too far. The ripples then draw the boat back within reach.

His rod and His staff are of inestimable comfort. I liken His rod to His Word. The Word of God can be used both offensively and defensively, either to keep us in line or to pull us back in line. It can be used for detection by the Shepherd to see if there is anything wrong with us or, on a more positive note, to see that all is well.

We are probably more familiar with the shepherd's staff. At times all this was used for was a gentle tap to remind the sheep that he is present. At other times, the shepherd's staff serves a more functional purpose when the crooked end is used to go around the neck of a sheep and pull it to safety.

I liken the staff unto the Spirit of God that dwells within His sheep. I grew up in the Episcopal Church at a time when this Spirit was referred to as the Holy Ghost. This term for the Spirit is still used in many church circles today. While it is a good term, I found it too spooky as a kid. Ghosts were not something by which to be comforted but scared of. Therefore I missed the value of God's Spirit. No wonder that when I first heard God's Spirit referred to as the Holy Spirit I liked the term better than *Ghost*.

In my estimation, the Holy Spirit is often the least mentioned and the least appreciated member of what is called the Trinity. I have come to see this as a grave error, for without the Holy Spirit we would not have the Scriptures (as the authors of Scripture were inspired to write what they wrote by Him); Mary could not have conceived of God's son, Jesus, the perfectly sinless God-Man (as what was conceived in Mary was by instrument of the Holy Spirit); and the process of God bringing a person to trust in the Shepherd is accomplished by the means of God's Spirit. Wow! Without the Holy Spirit, no Scriptures, no God coming to us in the flesh, no us coming to God.

God's Spirit is called the Comforter. Is it any wonder why? He, the Holy Spirit is my constant companion and comforter through the highs and lows of life. What He has secured for me, He will protect to see that I never lose—my salvation. While the journey of life may be risky, it is not a gamble. The rewards far outweigh the risks.

Enemies and Table Preparation

One of my favorite stories is that of a little boy who had badly misbehaved, for which the punishment in his family was that he could not eat at the family dining table. Instead, he was forced to sit and eat at a little table in the kitchen within sight of the family dining table. As he was about to eat, his father reminded him to say a blessing, to which he was heard to pray, "Thank You, Lord, that You have prepared a table for me in the presence of my enemies."

I remember early in life and early in marriage how long my mother and later my wife spent in the kitchen preparing meals. That observation doesn't even take into account the planning and purchasing of the meal before the actual preparation.

Sheep understand even less than I the meticulous preparation of the shepherd of the mesas or table lands on which they graze. Long before they ever sit down to eat so to speak, the shepherd has gone before them to prepare the mesa or table. What's to prepare? As I have previously written, green pastures just don't happen. Often the shepherd will seed a mesa. At other times he will check for snake holes and apply an ointment to the snake hole that repels them and drives them away. You see, sheep will literally stick their noses anywhere. Sound familiar? Furthermore, sheep will eat just about anything in front of them. Sound familiar?

Our appetites as people are not much more discriminating, and I'm not referring to just food. Just because it looks good doesn't mean it is good for us. Remember the fruit in the garden? Eve saw that it was good for food and pleasing to the eye, even though she knew it was forbidden. And you know the rest of the story. When will we learn?

There are also poisonous flowers and plants that, if consumed, will kill the sheep. The shepherd weeds them out.

Then when he leads his sheep to the table, viola! There it is! Dinner is ready, just like my dad, sister, and I experienced after mother slaved for hours in the kitchen; just like me, my son, and daughter experienced as we came to the table upon the call the dinner is ready. Little do we and the sheep know what painstaking care preceded the call to dinner.

Our Legacy

I performed a funeral several years ago. At its conclusion, I said good-bye to the son of the deceased. With his mother's eternal security freshly on my mind, I made some reference to eternal life, to which he responded that he believed that the only way we live on is through our children.

How sad if that's all there is. Like sheep, we have received mercy, but unlike sheep we have a consciousness to make a contribution, or give something back, and therefore we should leave a trail of mercy behind in appreciation for the mercy we have received in this life. Even though sheep are not conscious of the fact, they have been called those with golden hooves. Why? Wherever they go, they unknowingly leave a trail of goodness behind in terms of the way they beneficially fertilize the land. In my college fraternity, we made the commitment that we would leave the fraternity better than what we found it.

It has been my personal experience and observation that those who are others-centered are less stressed than those who are self-centered. There's something about giving out to others that takes the attention off oneself in a healthy way. There was an example of that in my small group last night. Larry Sherman and Brenda Smith just returned from a three-week trip to Namibia in Africa. This was Larry's eighth trip and Brenda's first. It was telling just to see the look on their faces as they spoke of caring for the poor, hungry little children scantily clothed. (They told of it being thirty degrees in the morning and seeing children with no shoes and sharing a pair of gloves). This is an AIDS-ridden culture in which the average lifespan is thirty-nine years of age. As we listened to their stories we could see how they were those with golden hooves as they were showing mercy and love by providing food, clothing, a sonogram machine, a brick making machine, computers, and teaching them to read. Larry goes back in November, and I'm sure Brenda will be returning very soon. I don't think it will be long before I go, either.

But you don't have to go half way around the world to show love and mercy. As the old saying goes: to love the world for me is no chore; the problem for me is loving my neighbor next door.

Another catchy little ditty:
You are writing a gospel every day
by the things you do
and the things you say.
People read what you write
distorted or true.
What is the gospel according to you?[4]
What will be your legacy?

Eternal Dwelling

Unlike sheep who are not concerned with what will happen to them when they die, we are made for an eternity, and we have the innate hope of living in a better place after this forever. This is not a place we deserve, nor a place we can create for ourselves.

I once had a woman come into my office with whom I spoke regarding her relationship to the Lord (inquiring if she trusted the Lord as her Shepherd). In all my days, I have never had a reaction like hers! When I asked her if she would like to place her trust in the Lord, she replied, "What's in it for me?" At first I was taken back, but the more I thought about it and the more I have continued to do so since that time, I think it is a fair question.

I then proceeded to enumerate the benefits to her (check out Song 103), and when I was through she was ready to sign on the dotted line. Much of what I enumerated to her is what I have been writing to you in this book.

Even if eternal life were not in the benefit package, I would sign up just for the earthly benefits of a personal relationship with the Lord as my Shepherd. To top it all off, "(Surely) I will dwell in the house of the Lord forever." The benefits are out of this world!

As I see it, here's how it all plays out in the end for those of us who have a personal relationship with Him while on this Earth.

If the Lord were to return today:

Those who have not placed their trust in Him as Shepherd will live an eternal existence where the influence of His caring presence will be absent.

Those who have died and have since been with Him in spirit form will accompany Him back.

Those of us who have placed our trust in Him as our Shepherd during this life will be joined with Him and them in a newly God-created Paradise similar, if not identical, to the original garden wherein we will live forever with Him and each other.

In this new earthly paradise, there will not be death, divorce, job firings, moving, disease of any kind, bankruptcies, hurricanes, competition, mosquitoes, lost handkerchiefs and socks, crime, rape, greed, lust, jealousy, selfishness, depression, discouragement, distress, or any thing else that cause us stress here on this present earth. Not to mention that men, women, and children will be safe in public alone.

This new earthly paradise will not only be marked by the absence of all those things that cause us stress, but it will be more positively marked by all the things that rightfully cause us joy here on this present earth, things like perfect love, joy, peace, patience, kindness, goodness, faithfulness, and self-control.

Eternal life will be one long holiday spent with the One for whom our important holidays (Christmas and Easter) are celebrated and without the stress of our current holidays.

I Shall Lack Nothing

I love what I read some time ago about a little girl who misquoted Psalm 23, but in her misquoting it never got it so right as when she said, "The Lord is my Shepherd; He's all I want."

The idea expressed here in David's song is that *if* the Lord is my Shepherd, then I shall not be in want. I will lack nothing or have want for anything other than what He provides, as that will be satisfyingly enough. As the little girl said, He's all I want.

Whatever good the world has to offer (and it has a lot of good to offer), it will never completely and permanently satisfy. What the world has to offer will always leave you wanting more and trying to hold on to what you've got. That's stressful.

The reasons for one being able to make the claim in the second part of the first clinching statement in this Song, "I shall lack nothing," is found in the subsequent assurances (vv. 2–6):

He makes me lie down in green pastures,
he leads me beside quiet waters,
he restores my soul.
He guides me in paths of righteousness for his name's
sake.
Even though I walk through the valley of the shadow
of death, I will fear no evil, for you are with me; your
rod and your staff, they comfort me.
You prepare a table before me in the presence of my
enemies.
You anoint my head with oil;
my cup overflows.
Surely goodness and love will follow me all the days
of my life,
and I will dwell in the house of the Lord forever.

Who is the Shepherd? The New Testament identifies Jesus
with the Shepherd of Song 23 in the Old Testament. Jesus is
stretching out His arms right now and speaking these words
to you:

Come to me, all you who are weary and burdened, and
I will be you rest. Take my yoke upon you and learn
from me, for I am gentle and humble in heart, and you
will find rest for your souls.

The world says to us, Come to me, and I will give you
stress. Jesus says, "Come to me...and I will give you rest"
(Matt. 11:28).

Who will you come to?

Afterword
Back to the Stressmores

I had the pleasure of joining the Stressmores for dinner at The Garden restaurant for what has become their weekly date night. You'd be pleased to know that they have taken these suggestions to heart, and while they wanted me to tell you that they still experience stress in their lives, they do now stress less.

Both Chris and Pat agree that among the many changes they have made in their lives, working personally on their relationship with the Shepherd (both in reading the Bible and praying on a fairly regular basis) has made the biggest difference. Attending church regularly also has enhanced their relationship. In addition, they joined a small group that meets weekly in the home of one of the members of their church. Their group has proven to be an invaluable source of encouragement and support. Chris continues to meet with Dale once a month for lunch for mutual accountability. Pat now meets weekly with one of the women in her small group.

The Stressmores faithfully review both of their budgets (one for how they spend their time and the other for how they spend their money) on their date nights closest to the first of every month.

Chris is back to jogging every other morning before work, and while it requires him to get up an hour earlier, the off-setting benefits of being in shape, sleeping better, and feeling his mind being sharper are well worth the sacrifice. Pat's new escape is a girl's night out with some of the women in her small group. To conserve time, she meets with her accountability partner from the small group for a half hour before they get together with the others.

Although neither Pat nor Chris ever made intimacy a part of their plan, they are both pleasantly surprised with the way their intimacy (physically and spiritually) has picked up. They attribute the open, honest, and frequent communication to this refreshing dynamic that they thought was lost forever in their relationship. Pat tells her accountability partner that things haven't been this way between Chris and her since dating days.

As a family they are doing better, but this continues to be the biggest struggle to juggle everyone's schedule so that they can have some family time together. The two greatest accomplishments have been striving for at least three nights together at home for dinner. This has done more to improve family communication than anything else they've tried.

Having Chris's mother come to live with them has turned out better than expected, largely due to a major sit down meeting at the very beginning to talk through everyone's expectations and concerns. In addition, they all agreed to sit down for an honest review every quarter, or more frequently if desirable.

Work wise, things are just about the same. Some things you just can't change. Having said that, however, both seem to be handling work-related stress better, simply as a result of having stressed less in some of the other areas of their lives.

Conclusion

Stress is a mess! And do you know what that makes us when we are stressed? Messed!

Stress negatively affects our mind, body, and spirit.

While we cannot completely eliminate stress, we can and should seek the means of reducing stress and learning to cope with what we cannot reduce any further. So:

Identify the stressors in your life.

Identify the symptoms of stress in your life.

Identify the steps of reducing or coping with your stress.

Place your trust in Jesus as your Shepherd to care for you and guide you in reducing your stress and learning better to cope with your stress.

And come sing with me and the Stressmores the song of the stressed less.

End Notes

Preface

1. Dr. Sam Peeples, Jr., "Stress Management Seminar," Christian Ministries, Inc., Birmingham, Alabama.
2. Ibid.
3. Material obtained from http://www.new-oceans.co.uk, accessed July 21, 2008.

Part I: Leading Stressors

Chapter 1

1. ABC's *World News Tonight*, "The Money Trap," July 11, 2006.
2. *Orlando Sentinel*, July 24, 2006.

Chapter 3

1. Jeffery Deaver, *Cold Moon* (New York: Simon & Schuster, 2006), 47.
2. ABC's *World News Tonight*, July 11, 2006.

Part II: Leading Symptoms

Chapter 4

1. MacDonald Consultants, healthyworkplaceweek.ca, accessed September 1, 2008.

Chapter 5

1. MacDonald Consultants, healthyworkplaceweek.ca.
2. Dr. Sam Peeples, Jr., "Stress Management Seminar," Christian Ministries, Inc., Birmingham, Alabama.
3. Claudia Wallis, "Stress," *Time*, June 6, 1983, 49–54.

Chapter 6

1. MacDonald Consultants, healthyworkplaceweek.ca.
2. David W. Smith, *The Friendless American Male* (Ventura, CA: Regal Books, 1983).

3. "The Touch of the Master's Hand" by John Kramp. Copyright © 1976 by Paragon Music (ASCAP) (Administered by Brentwood-Benson Music Publishing, Inc.). All rights reserved. Used by permission.

Part III: Leading Solutions

Chapter 8

1. Gordon MacDonald, *Ordering Your Private World* (Nashville, TN: Thomas Nelson, 2007).

2. Charles Hummel, *The Tyranny of the Urgent* (Downers Grove, IL: 1999).

3. Ibid.

Chapter 9

1. Jon Krakauer, *Into the Wild* (New York: Anchor Books, Random House, 1996), 189.

2. Ibid.

3. Ibid.

Chapter 10

1. Kate Santich, "Pause and push 'refresh,'" *Orlando Sentinel*, July 8, 2006, D3.

2. Ibid.

3. Ibid.

Chapter 11

1. Jane Bryant Quinn, "A Debit-Card Nation," *Newsweek*, July 31, 2006, 45.

2. Gregory Karp, "Don't hit the skids after hitting the big jackpot," *Orlando Sentinel*, September 3, 2006, G2.

Chapter 12

1. Philip Keller, *A Shepherd Looks at Psalm 23* (Grand Rapids, MI: Zondervan, 1970).

2. Reid Hanley, "Wie finds trouble," *Orlando Sentinel*, July 14, 2006, D3.

3. Ibid.

4. From Web site: www.ultreya-solutions.com/sayings.htm, accessed October 3, 2008.

About the Author

The author is a native Floridian who currently lives in Central Florida with his wife, Linda, and daughter, Ann. The Montgomerys also have a son, Fletcher; daughter-in-law, Sarah; and two teenage grandsons, Nicholas and Michael, who live in South Carolina.

Dr. Montgomery graduated from Florida State University (F.S.U.). Even still, he has many University of Florida friends who will want to read this book, as Montgomery is not a Gator-hater nor does he root against the Gators, except for on one stress-filled Saturday afternoon each year in late November. Therefore this book is for Seminoles, Gators, and stress-filled people everywhere.

Upon graduation from F.S.U. in 1963, Dr. Montgomery spent eight years in the banking business in Atlanta, Georgia, then moved to his hometown, Coral Gables, Florida, to take over a family building supply business, which was sold several years later when he entered seminary. For the last thirty-plus years he has served as the pastor of churches in Minneapolis, Atlanta, and Lake Mary, Florida, where he currently serves the River Oaks Presbyterian Church (PCA).

To Contact the Author

John Montgomery
Senior Pastor
RiverOaks Church
(407) 333-9103
john@riveroakschurch.com